From Sting to Spin
A History of Nettle Fibre

GILLIAN EDOM

From Sting to Spin - A History of Nettle Fibre

ISBN 978-0-9565693-1-8

First published in the United Kingdom in 2010 by Urtica Books,

97 Hewarts Lane, Bognor Regis, West Sussex, PO21 3DJ.

Revised Edition published 2019

Copyright © Gillian Edom 2010

Printed by Book Printing UK

The right of Gillian Edom to be identified as the author of this work has been asserted by her in accordance with the Copyright, Designs and Patents Act 1988.

All rights reserved. No part of this publication may be produced in any form or by any means – graphic, electronic or mechanical including photocopying, recording, taping or information storage and retrieval systems, without the prior permission, in writing, of the publisher.

A CIP catalogue record of this book can be obtained from the British Library.

Editing and design: John Edom.

Cover photo: Allan Brown.

All other photos are by the author unless otherwise stated.

Preface to the Second Edition

When this book was first published in 2010, I underestimated the worldwide and enduring interest in the subject of nettle fibre use and so the relatively small quantity of printed copies soon ran out. There were many changes that I wanted to make to the book so over the last few years I have attempted to correct and revise a new edition. The birth of the Nettles for Textiles Facebook group in 2017 and its rapid growth inspired me to complete the task, and as I have followed the posts during the last year or so, it has become apparent that the possibility of extracting useable fibre from nettles, particularly on an artisanal scale, is greater than I could ever have imagined. This groundswell of people all around the world doing it for themselves, of course substantiates the nettle's historical use for textile fibre. The Nettles for Textiles group has also been a platform for people around the world to share their knowledge of localised nettle fibre use from the past, and their own varied yet successful techniques for extracting it. The scope of this information would have been very difficult for one individual to track down before the emergence of social media. There is also increased availability of online historic and archival resources, saving many hours of travelling and sitting in reading rooms and libraries. As a result, the emergence of so much new material, as well as better access to original sources, may provide new and differing conclusions to those reached in this book, which is excellent news. My aim was never to write a definitive work on nettle fibre use but to collate all the information that I had found in the hope that it would be taken forward and added to as new information was uncovered.

It is certain that ongoing research and experimentation will continue to shed new light on the historical use of nettle fibre. Improved technology will enable easier identification of archaeological textile fibres and the worldwide sharing of ideas and techniques for extracting the fibre will consolidate the rather patchy existing knowledge of its historical use. My enduring hope is that the growing body of knowledge relating to nettle fibre will greatly increase the possibility of it affording an alternative, more sustainable source of natural fibre at a time when the world so desperately needs it.

Foreword

Early in childhood we soon learn how to recognise stinging nettles. Thereafter we tend to avoid or ignore them. But over the centuries nettles have contributed a great deal to the wellbeing of humankind, and in recent times there has been a revival of interest in this common, widespread and easily recognisable species.

With the Transition Town Movement and similar initiatives people are looking again at local native plants and re-evaluating their uses, particularly as food. Throughout the British Isles there was a widespread belief that three meals of stinging nettles each spring would 'cleanse the blood' and ensure good health throughout the year. In rural areas nettle beer was a favourite drink. Nettles played an important role in cottagers' lives.

Now at the opening of a new century a new cottage industry has emerged: the writing of books on nettles. This book is the fourth book to be produced in recent years, and, like the earlier ones, it is self-published, so its production can be considered to be the 21st century equivalent of a cottage industry. Of the earlier three publications, two attempt to stimulate a general interest in nettles, and the third deals with the plant's folklore and traditional uses in the British Isles. Gillian Edom's book is the result of many years' research on nettles, and, particularly, her tireless investigations into the production and uses of nettle fibres. Of the four books written so far, it is the most thorough and the most scholarly, giving a masterful overview of her subject. No doubt there is a great deal more to be discovered and I hope that Gillian's work will excite others to seek out and record other samples of nettle cloth. Even if readers don't accept this challenge, I hope they will, like me, be encouraged to look anew at a plant which is both very ordinary and, at the same time, very extraordinary.

When we discover the extraordinary in the everyday and the ordinary, we begin to reconnect with and truly appreciate our local environment.

Roy Vickery
South London Botanical Institute
April 2010

Introduction to First and Revised Editions and Acknowledgements

This book is the result of many years of research and distractions from research. It all began because I discovered some years ago that nobody appeared to have written a 'proper' book about nettles. I naively decided this was something I could do myself, but my research took on a life of its own and I found myself becoming more and more fascinated by the use of nettles as a fibre source. During this period other books have been published on nettles, which was a great relief because it meant that I could concentrate on the aspect of nettles that interested me the most.

I have examined the history of the use of nettle fibre from a northern European perspective, while at the same time trying to give an overview of the range of fibre yielding plants that exist in the *Urticaceae* family worldwide. Even so, I am conscious that what I have discovered and documented in this book is only the tip of the iceberg. I am aware that there is a wealth of literature in Scandinavia, Germany, France and Russia, to give but a few examples, on the use of *Urtica dioica* – in particular – as a source of fibre. Were this literature to be studied in detail as a whole, the historical picture of nettle fibre use would be more complete.

The time period of history covered within this book ranges from prehistoric times to the Second World War. After the war, raw materials for textiles became abundant and so there was no further demand for attempts to revive traditional skills to meet shortages. Research into the cultivation of nettles and extraction and processing of fibre during the last twenty or more years reflects the desire to apply modern technology to a forgotten art and to produce a more sustainable textile raw material. This is a new era, with new challenges and evolved capabilities.

It would not be possible to list every individual person who has assisted me in some way during the research and writing of the first edition of this book, but each of the following played an essential part. I would particularly like to thank Laura Hastings who worked at the Royal Botanical Gardens in Kew and dedicated a huge amount of time to helping and supporting me during the first few years of my research. I am sure I would have given up long ago had it not been for her enthusiasm. Also, Dr. Jens Dreyer in Hamburg – a key figure in the world of nettle fibre. He took great interest in my work and gave me a huge amount of assistance. It was an honour to have his support.

There are other key people who helped and advised me in a variety of ways over many years and I am extremely grateful to them: Anne Batzer, John and Thelma Beswick, Dr. Jane Harwood, Professor Ray Harwood, Dr. Eva Koch, Dr. Ulla Mannering, Christina Stapley, Kristen Thorrud, Roy Vickery, Dennis Waldron, Caroline Ware, Dr. John Peter Wild and Terry Couchman.

I would like to thank Dr. Annabelle Hughes, Dr. Susanna Harris and Des Pawson for providing further information that I was able to include in this new edition.

Special thanks to Allan Brown and Brigitte Kaltenbacher, who now hold a key place in 'nettle world'. Allan has become highly skilled at nettle fibre extraction and has shared his valuable knowledge through short films and by founding the Nettles for

Textiles Facebook Group. He also kindly permitted me to use one of his photos of his own extracted nettle fibre for the cover of this book. Brigitte, a weaver and textile researcher, is also a nettle fibre enthusiast and compiler of the Nettles for Textiles website. They have both given their advice and support, and most importantly their encouragement.

Finally I would like to thank my son John Edom for kindly and generously giving up so much time to proofread, edit and design this second edition. I'm not only very grateful, but proud of him as well.

To Elijah, Dulcie, Mary, Olive, Phoebe and Jonah.

Contents

Preface to the Second Edition

Foreword

Introduction to First and Revised Editions and Acknowledgements

Introduction	2
Nettle archaeology: ancient traces of nettle fibre use	10
Nettle ethnobotany: the use of nettle fibre by indigenous communities around the world	22
Nettle fibre in Japan	32
Early records: the use of nettle fibre in Europe	40
Fibre found in fairy tales	52
The Wild Swans: Hans Christian Andersen's version	55
Attempts to commercialise nettle fibre	60
Where is nettlecloth today?	72
A future for nettle fibre?	88
A basic guide to fibre extraction	92
Index	97

... and every year in the port of Orissa were laden five and twenty or thirty ships great and small ... of cloth of herbs, which is a kind of silk which groweth amongst the woods without any labour of man. [Marginal note: This cloth we call Nettle cloth.]

Richard Hakluyt, *Volume 09 Asia, Part II*, 1599

Therebe (sic) of Plants, which they use for Garments, these that follow: Hempe, flax, cotton, nettles (whereof they make nettlecloth) ...

Francis Bacon, *Sylva Sylvarum*, 1631

It is another question whether the word linen be not a much older one in Europe, known there before the introduction of flax, and signifying fibre in general, and the stuffs knitted or woven from it. Fishing with the line or the net is a very primitive occupation, and even savages know how to twist fibres and plant flexible matting from all kinds of nettle-plants and from the bast of certain trees.

Victor Hehn, *The wanderings of plants and animals from their first home*, 1888

In the Pyrenees it was the custom of women to carry stems in bags under their skirts, so that the heat of the body might perform the retting process, after which it was necessary only to break the core and shake out the wood.

F. I. Oakley, *Long Vegetable fibres*, 1928

Introduction

The Stinging Nettle. A plant we love to hate and probably one of the most widely written about wild plants in the whole of Europe. Human beings and nettles have a symbiotic relationship: the former produce waste rich in nitrates and phosphates, which in turn stimulate the latter's growth. As a result the nettle has benefited from people, while people have benefited from the nettle, making use of its huge range of properties. Throughout history mankind has used nettles as food and fodder, in medicine, for cordage and, of course, in textiles. In addition to their practical uses, nettles have also found their way into our mythology, folklore, language and literature.

The growth of nettles is further stimulated when soil is disturbed, which means they may be indicators of previous human activity. Long forgotten settlements are often marked by dense nettle growth. One example is Little Gidding in Huntingdonshire, deserted during the 17th century but where, more than two hundred years later, tall nettles were reported to mark the abandoned area.[1]

Rumour, hearsay and the quest for nettle fibre

Much has been written about the use of nettle fibre to produce textiles. Unfortunately, some of this writing is based on assumption and rumour. For example, it has been said that King

---

1 Rackham, Oliver, 1986, *The History of the Countryside*, Phoenix Giant, p 109.

Henry VIII had a favourite nettle fibre shirt, that Queen Elizabeth I wore nettle fibre underwear and that Mary Queen of Scots preferred to sleep in nettle fibre sheets. It is quite possible that these statements contain some truth, though I have been unable to find any evidence to support these claims.

In 2002 a new rumour found its way into the public domain: an Italian fashion company planned to produce a shirt made from nettle fibre and as part of a publicity campaign distributed branded packets of stinging nettle seeds. On the reverse of the packet it was written that nettle fibre was used to make the uniforms of Napoleon's soldiers, and of course, this particular statement was quickly taken up by the media. During the several years I had been researching nettles up to this point, this was the first time the story had come to my attention. When I contacted the company to find out the original source of the information, they were unable to remember. To investigate further, I contacted the Musée de l'Armée in Paris, and was informed that Napoleonic uniforms had been made from wool, linen or cotton.[2]

Evidently this cannot be taken as the final word on the matter. Who knows? There may be evidence somewhere that could shine further light on Napoleonic nettle fibre uniforms and we should therefore remain open minded. However, as much of my research has shown, the quest to produce textiles from nettle fibre – such a bountiful and sustainable natural resource – has given rise to periodic instances of rumour – or even propaganda – that appear to offer hope for a successful extraction process or a bona fide historical precedent that might inform how nettle fibre extraction

---

2 Chaduc, Lieutenant-Colonel Gérard-Jean, Conservateur du département XIXème siècle, Musée de l'Armée, Paris, Personal communication by letter 13th September 2002, *Règlement sur l'habillement des Troupes de l'Armée de Terre*, 1812.

could be implemented today. Sometimes the story is simply too good to be true.

When assessing any reference to past nettle fibre use, it should not always be taken at face value. It is necessary to have an understanding of historical and geographical context. For example, if other plant or animal fibres were more readily available, what could be the reason for choosing to use nettle? Also, what imports were coming into the country at the time? Could it be that an imported fibre from a foreign species of nettle was being used?

The broader Nettle Family

The word 'nettle' itself can be misleading. There are currently around 1,500 plant species worldwide that belong to the Nettle Family (*Urticaceae*), of which the common stinging nettle, *Urtica dioica*, native to western Europe is just one.[3] A variety of fibre yielding nettles belonging to other *Urticaceae* genera such as *Laportea*, *Girardinia* and *Boehmeria* grow throughout the world. These plants can be described as nettles, but they are not the same plant as the nettle species we see growing profusely around us in northern Europe. Therefore, when the word 'nettle' is used, it is important to identify exactly which plant is being referred to.

Links between textile terms and the word 'nettle'

The etymology of the word 'nettle' is linked with several words that have a connection with textiles. It is possible that fibres from nettles were used to make the earliest of threads, and that nets – used for hunting and fishing – were the earliest form of textiles.

---

3   *The Plant List* (2013). Version 1.1. Published on the Internet; http://www.theplantlist.org/ (accessed 23rd November 2017).

The Latin *nere* means 'to spin' and *necto* means 'to tie, bind or weave'. The Sanskrit *nah* means 'to bind'. The Greek *nein* means 'to spin' and *nen* gives rise to the English net, needle and nettle. The Germanic branch of the Indo-European family of languages has a very clear pattern of words that derive from the root *ne* or *nen*. The nettle and the development of early textile technologies can thus be considered to be closely intertwined.

New discoveries

In the first edition of this book I included a reference to 'nettlecloth' being used to describe a type of cordage found in the *Sailor's Pocket Book* of 1877.[4]

In fact, the term used in the pocket book was not 'nettlecloth', but 'nettle stuff'. The use of the word Nettle, Nittle or Knittle to define a particular type of cordage has a long history, and Des Pawson, a leading authority on knots and sailor's rope-work, kindly sent me several references to illustrate this. There are various descriptions relating to 'nettle stuff':

> …two rope yarns twisted together in a knot at each end, to seize a rope, or block or like.

'The Seaman's Dictionary' (first circulated as a manuscript in 1620-23) in Manwayring, G. E. & Perrin. W. G. (eds.), *The Life and Works of Sir Henry Manwayring, Vol II*, 1922, London: Navy Records Society, London.

> A small line, which is either plaited or twisted, and used for various purposes at sea; as to fasten the service on the cable, to reef the sails by the bottom, and to hang the hammocks between decks; this name is also given to the loops or buttons of a bonnet (a kind of sail).

4 Bedford, Sir Frederick George Denham, 1877, *The Sailor's Pocket Book. A collection of practical rules, notes, and tables,* Griffin & Co., Portsmouth.

Needle		Nettle		To Sew or Spin	
German	*nadel*	German	*nessel*	German	*nähen*
Dutch	*naald*	Dutch	*netel*	Dutch	*naaien*
Swedish	*nål*	Swedish	*nässla*	Swedish	*sy*
Icelandic	*nal*	Danish	*nædle*		
Middle English	*needle*				
Old English	*nædl*	Old English	*netele (to twist, derived from noedle meaning needle)*	Old English	*simian*
Anglo Saxon	*noedel*	Anglo Saxon	*netele, netle*		
		Old High German	*nazza*	Old High German	*siuwen*
				Latin	*suere*
				Sanskrit	*siv*

Falconer, William, 1780, *An* (sic) *Universal Dictionary of the Marine*, London: Printed for T. Cadell

Nettles – small line used for seizings, and for hammock clues.

Smythe, Admiral W. H., 1867, *The Sailor's Word Book: An Alphabetical Digest of Nautical Terms, including Some More Especially Millitary and Scientific, but Useful to Seamen; as well as Archaisms of Early Voyagers, etc.*, Blackie and Son.

Interestingly, a knittle or knotted cord was issued to sailors to whip a miscreant who was sentenced to 'run the gauntlet' (*The Sailor's Word Book*).

I found this misunderstanding on my part extremely interesting, and came to two conclusions. Firstly, of the importance of making efforts to trace back the etymology of a word to its earliest appearance, if that is at all possible. We often discover how interlinked the various activities that have a connection to this word are. Secondly, how easy it is to interpret the meaning of historical words according to our 21st century experience and understanding: we are prone to making assumptions.[5]

---

[5] My thanks to Des Pawson for his gracious letter providing me with this important information.

With what materials may the Sabbath lamp be lighted, and with what may it not be lighted? It may not be lighted with cedar-bast, nor with uncombed flax, nor with floss-silk, nor with willow-fibre, nor with nettle fibre, nor with waterweeds ...

Mishnah, Treatise Sabbath, ch. Ii, *The Standard Prayer Book*, tr. Simeon Singer. [1915]

It is only in recent years that a purpose has been found for which ramie is superior to all other fibres; viz; the manufacture of gas mantles, and to this work is now almost exclusively devoted.

F. I. Oakley, *Long Vegetable fibres*, 1928

Nettle archaeology: ancient traces of nettle fibre use

How often were nettles used as a textile fibre in the past? We shall probably never have a satisfactory answer to this question because the evidence, in the form of archaeological discoveries, written records, literature, folklore and the claims of eyewitnesses in more recent history, is limited. Nettles would have been one of a number of wild native plants used as a textile fibre or as cordage by early communities before the emergence of cultivated crops and wool. Our ancestors developed a variety of skills to create fabric, from plaiting, twisting and netting during the Palaeolithic era to more complicated techniques for textile production as time went on, including spinning, weaving and felting. It is easy to imagine how the use of nettle fibre came about: broken nettle stems left lying on the ground would have started to decompose. Once the soft outer skin of the stem began to break down, the layer of fibres would detach from the central core of the stem and become visible. We might be unlikely to notice this process today, but those whose existence depended on an intimate knowledge of their immediate environment certainly would have. Of course, it is not possible to know precisely when and how nettle fibres were first stumbled upon, but for those who have handled them themselves, it is easy to imagine the possibilities.

There have been very few archaeological finds that have been identified as being made from *Urtica dioica* fibre. There may be several explanations for this:

♦   Any archaeological samples of nettle fibre textiles found can only be representative. It is likely that nettle fibre was used widely for cordage and textiles throughout pre-history. In our fast-changing age it is sometimes easy to forget that ideas and practices once evolved at a much slower pace. Traditional practices were much more deeply rooted and less easily overturned. With respect to nettle fibre, textile historian and curator at the National Museum of Denmark Margrethe Hald[6] made an interesting observation about its use by peasant cultures. Until as late as the beginning of the 20th century, these communities were often completely untouched by post-industrial influences and it was her opinion that their traditions and culture often reflected far more ancient practices. She gave the example of the Ostjak and Wogul people of Siberia, who used thread made from the tendons of animals and nets made of nettle fibre as late as 1904. A further example is The Ice Man (Ötzi), discovered in 1991 in a glacier in the Ötztaler Alps on the border between Austria and Italy and dated to have lived during the Neolithic Period.[7] The outer garment he wore at the time of his death was a plaited grass cloak. In approximately 1729-30, a traveller in Turin recorded seeing local people wearing straw or reed cloaks of a very similar appearance. These examples illustrate the persistent use of certain technologies and materials without significant change throughout long periods. Confirmed archaeological finds of nettle fibre are thus likely to reflect further examples of an ongoing traditional practice.

6   Hald, M., 1980, *Ancient Danish Textiles from Bogs and Burials*, The National Museum of Denmark, pp. 126-127.
7   Spindler, K., 1993, *The Man in the Ice*, Weidenfeld and Nicolson, London, p. 146.

♦ In the past, preservation of textile remains was not given the highest priority by archaeologists, therefore much may have been lost through ignorance or neglect. Happily, the importance of textile study is receiving increased recognition within the field of archaeology, giving rise to the development of new or improved technologies for their identification, analysis and preservation as well as innovative approaches in experimental archaeology.

♦ Compared to animal fibres, plant fibres deteriorate very quickly. Surviving textile samples therefore tend to be few, small and in poor condition.

♦ It has always been difficult to distinguish between individual flax and nettle fibre cells because of their similarity. As more accurate methods of fibre identification are developed, it is possible that some archaeological textiles previously identified as flax may eventually prove to be nettle.[8]

♦ The extraction of the fibre from nettles is more intensive – and painful – than that of fibres from flax, for example. While nettles would have grown abundantly around human settlements, as other plant fibres became available these might have been used in preference to nettle. This is particularly likely to have been the case if, as with flax, it was possible to cultivate this alternative as a crop. On the other hand,

---

8   Since the first publication of this book in 2010 there have been developments in this field, as demonstrated by recent investigations into the Lusehøj Bronze Age textile from Voldofte in Denmark. Bergfjord, C. et al, 2012, 'Nettle as a distinct bronze age textile plant', *Scientific Reports*, vol 2, no. 664, pp. 1-4. DOI: 10.1038/srep00664.

the cultivation of plants such as flax would have been time consuming and labour intensive in itself, while nettles look after their own growth, requiring little to no attention.

The sum total of finds identified as nettle fibre throughout Europe are few and so provide little evidence of its very early use, though are interesting examples in themselves and precious for their scarcity.

The Sweet Track Find

The earliest dated example of nettle fibre in an archaeological find is possibly the Sweet Track arrowhead binding, which was found, along with other items, by peat cutter Ray Sweet in 1970. The Somerset Levels track was built between 4000 and 3500 BC as a raised path across a wet reed swamp. Studies of the site have enabled archaeologists to paint an interesting picture of the lives of the people who walked this path so many years ago. In comparison to other Neolithic sites, there were very few arrowheads found. Amongst those that were, however, one was still attached to a section of its hazelwood shaft. Some fibres were attached to the split shaft, on the surface of which were what appeared to be the bases of stinging nettle hairs.[9] It is unusual to find an arrowhead with a plant fibre binding and its identification as nettle fibre is a strong likelihood. The strips of bast and fibre may have been peeled away from the nettle stalks and used in this rough and raw state to bind the arrowhead to the shaft. Bushcraft specialist Ray Mears has shown how effective this method of binding can be by

---

9   Coles, J. M., Hibbert, F. A. and Orme, B. J., 1973, Prehistoric Roads and Tracks in Somerset: 3. The Sweet Track Proceedings of the Prehistoric Society, 39, p. 291.

developing a simple method of using nettle stalks to make cordage. The outer bast of the skin with the fibres attached is removed from the inner core of the stem and twisted to make string, requiring no complex fibre extraction process, nor tools, and can thus be carried out 'on the hoof'.[10]

The Funnelbeaker Sherd

In Denmark a clay sherd bearing a fine textile imprint was found at the Slotshøj-megalith at Stege. This fragment of pottery dates from approximately 2900 to 3000 BC and is believed to belong to the Funnelbeaker Culture. This Copper Age culture was well known for creating fine ceramics and using textiles to ornament work. Though unfortunately none of the threads on this particular piece of clay have survived, it is still possible to see that the fine fibre was derived from a plant. In 1980 Margrethe Hald rejected the likelihood of the fibre being from flax because, at the time of writing, there was no evidence of flax fibre use in Denmark so early in pre-history. The first discovery of fabric made from flax was dated to the early Iron Age (400 BC onwards).[11] The possibility of the sherd fibre being nettle is unfortunately one that cannot be proved because fibre identification can only take place if the fibre itself has been preserved.

Whitehorse Hill Bronze Age Burial

In 2011, an Early Bronze Age cist containing cremated human remains and dated to between 1730 –1600 BC, was excavated at Whitehorse Hill on Dartmoor. The ornaments accompanying the

10 Mears, R., 1995, August, *Bushcraft*, BBC Wildlife, Vol 13, No. 8, p.14.
11 Hald 1980.

burial suggest the burial chamber belonged to a young woman. A composite textile and animal skin item was found inside the chamber and identified as a panel of finely woven nettle fibre with two edges of decorative leather. This had been laid over a bed of plant material and the cremated remains, wrapped in a bear pelt and placed on top. It is uncertain what the original use of the textile had been, but it was of a high quality of craftsmanship and the many hours it would have taken to make indicate that it may have been a prestigious item. It is possible that the woven piece may have included other species of plant fibre, but the only fibres tested proved to be nettle (*Urtica dioica*).[12]

The Beeston Regis I Hoard

In 1979, James Ellis, a pupil at Beeston Hall School in Norfolk, discovered a Late Bronze Age hoard in the school playing fields while treasure hunting with his metal detector. Amongst the hoard were several socketed axes and remnants of string. In 1981, some of the string was positively identified as bast fibres from the stem of the stinging nettle, *Urtica dioica*, twisted to form a cord. The find dates to a period between 1100 and 900 BC. As with the Sweet Track Find, we should not be surprised to find evidence of the use of nettle bast and fibre as cordage during the Bronze Age.[13,14,15]

---

12 Jones, A. M., 2017, *Preserved in the Peat: An Extraordinary Bronze Age Burial on Whitehorse Hill, Dartmoor, and its Wider Context*, Oxbow Books
13 The dating of the Bronze Age period in Britain varies but is commonly considered to cover the period from 2750 BC to 650 BC.
14 Lawson, A. J., 1980b. 'A late Bronze Age hoard from Beeston Regis, Norfolk' *Antiquity* 54, 217-9 and plates 28-9.
15 Cutler, D., 1981, 14th January, Letter to Mr. A. Lawson, Norfolk Archaeological Unit.

The Voldofte Grave Cloth

The best known prehistoric example of a nettle textile is the Lusehøj textile from a tomb discovered in Voldofte in the district of Baag in Denmark during the 19th century. A piece of cloth was found wrapped around some cremated human bones in an urn placed in the tomb. The grave dated from Period V of the Scandinavian Late Bronze Age, between 900 and 750 BC. Textile archaeologists at the time of the find thought the cloth to have been made from flax fibres and saw it as evidence of flax cultivation in Denmark during the early Bronze Age. However, analysis by Danish botanist and ecologist Dr. Mogens Køie[16] during the middle of the last century revealed that it was in fact nettle fibre. This conclusion has been supported by recent studies that measure the fibrillar orientation of the fibres using polarised light microscopy and verify the presence of calcium oxalate crystals in association with the fibres.[17] The cloth was originally finely spun and contained 12 to 18 threads per centimetre and is s/s spun and woven in tabby. These analyses of the cloth also enabled its identification as being made from nettles that had grown in the Kärnten-Steiermark region in Austria.[18] It has been suggested that its status as an imported textile to an area where similar raw materials were available may indicate that nettle textiles were luxury items.

---

16 Køie, M., 1943, 'Clothing from Younger Bronze Age Made By Nettles', *Yearbook for Nordic Antiquarianism*. See also: Hald, M., 1942, 'The Nettle as a Culture Plant', *Folkliv*, Vol 6, pp. 28-49; and, Geijer, A., 1979, *A History of Textile Art*, Pasold Research Fund, London, p.10.
17 Bergfjord, C. et al., 2012. Nettle as a distinct Bronze Age textile plant. Scientific Reports, 2(1). Available at: http://dx.doi.org/10.1038/srep00664.
18 Ibid.

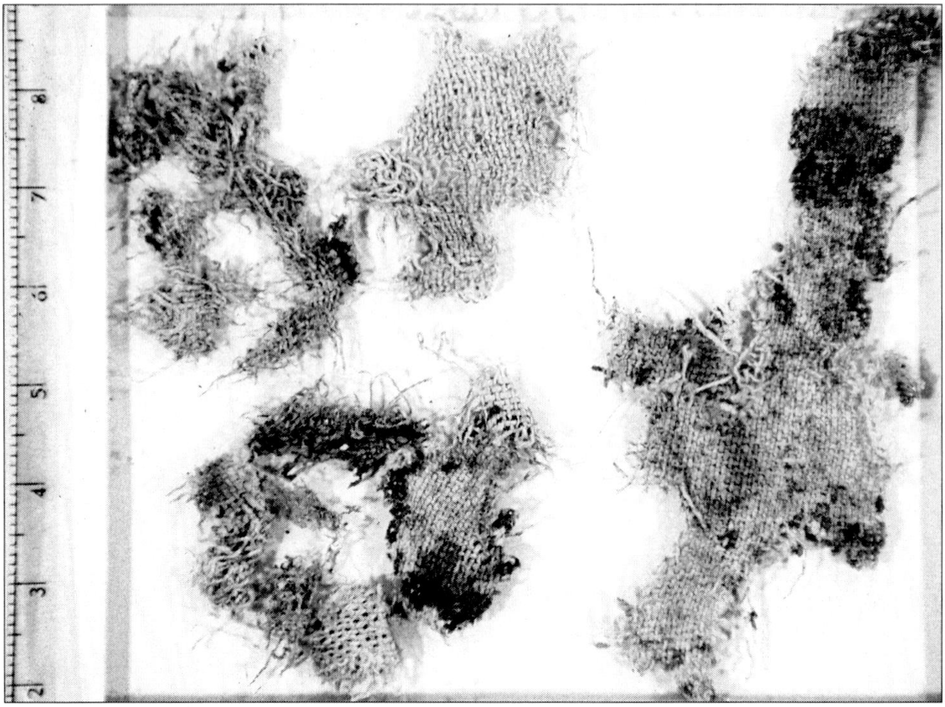

The Voldofte grave nettle fibre find (used with kind permission of the National Museum of Denmark, Copenhagen)

Tabby weave pattern

The Kvalsund Boat

During the same period of history as the Voldofte burial, a bundle of nettle stems was placed close to a pre-Viking longboat at Kvalsund in Norway. The boat was discovered in 1929 and carbon dated to approximately 680 BC. It is likely to have been a rowing boat as there was no evidence of a sail, mast or mast mounting. The nettle stems appeared to have been gathered, prepared for retting and placed deliberately, a conclusion supported by the fact that the surrounding environment – a peat bog – was not favourable to the growth of nettles.[19]

The Nørre Sandegaard Grave

Another Danish discovery, dating from the Late Iron Age (650-700AD), was made in a woman's grave at Nørre Sandegaard. Small lengths of finely spun yarn were found preserved by oxidation that had formed on the bronze sewing box that contained them. The lengths of yarn were all bound together in a row. Three of the skeins were woollen yarn and the fourth was spun from plant fibres. These were identified by Dr. Mogens Køie as nettle fibre in 1943.[20]

Nettlecloth from Flurlingen

The first find of nettle fibre textiles from the Early Middle Ages was in a grave in Fluringen near Schiffhausen in Switzerland. The grave belonged to a young girl and was dated to around 700

---

19 Jessen, K., 1929, 'Nelden (*Urtica dioica L.*)' in *Kvalsund-Fundet, Bergens Museums Skrifter*, Vol 2.2.
20 Becker, C. J., 1953, 'Miscellanea: Zwei Frauengräber des 7 Jahrhunderts aus Nørre Sandegaard, Bornholm', *Acta Archaeologica* (Kobenhavn), Vol. 24 pp. 127-155.

AD. The fabric was attached to the buckle of a belt that the girl was wearing when buried and was identified as being of nettle fibre. It has been concluded that an undergarment of fine nettle cloth had been worn by the girl and that fragments of textile had been preserved through the oxidation of the metal.[21]

The Oseberg Burial Ship

The Oseberg burial ship in Norway was excavated by Professor Gabriel Gustafson in 1904. It is thought that this important archaeological discovery contained the remains of a queen who had died in around 680 AD. A large quantity of textiles was identified, 58 fragments of which were said to have been woven with wool and nettle fibre. Some samples appeared to have a nettle warp, though this had largely disintegrated, and a thick woollen weft. One sample was possibly woven with a wool and nettle warp and a thick weft of red wool. Unfortunately the site had been disturbed previously by grave robbers so it was difficult to identify the uses for which the textiles had originally been made.[22]

The Coppergate Find

Finally, amongst the small finds discovered at the Coppergate site in York were fifty two samples of cloth made from vegetable fibres. Most of these were in poor condition, but one stood apart

---

21 Windler, R., Rast-Eicher, A., 1995, 'Nessel und Flachs – Textilfunde aus einem frühmittelalterlichen Mädchengrab in Fluringen (Kanton Zürich)', *Archaeologie der Schweiz*, Vol 18, pp. 155-161.
22 Stine Ingstad, A., 1981, 'The Functional Textiles from the Oseberg Ship', in Bender Jorgenson, L., and Tidow, K., (eds.), *NESAT I: Textilsymposium Neumünster*.

from the rest and was identified as being nettle fibre.[23] The fabric dates from 930-975 AD. Although its identification is uncertain, in light of the ongoing tradition of nettle fibre use in Scandinavia, this tradition, or even the textile itself, might easily have been brought to England during the period of Nordic settlement of 865-896.

---

23   Walton, P., 1989, 'Textiles, Cordage and Raw Fibre from 16-22 Coppergate', *The Archaeology of York: The Small Finds*, Council for British Archaeology for the York Archaeological Trust.

On a warm day late in summer, when the stinging nettles have grown tall from moist air and rich earth, a small group of women cut the slender stems that tower over their heads. From the split and dried stalks their experienced hands prepare long fibres, spin the fibres into twine, and knot the twine into fish netting so strong it can lift a load of herring from the water into a canoe ...

H. H. Smith, Ethnobotany of the Ojibwe Indians, 1932

In the southern region, where Khanty live in small agricultural villages, clothing was traditionally made from hemp and nettles pounded, spun and woven into cloth. Berries, grass and tree roots were used for dyeing embroidery thread and other yarn.

J. Oakes and R. Riewe, Spirit of Siberia: Traditional Life, Clothing and Footwear, 1998

The indigenous population of southern Kamchatka is not numerous; just a few Kamchadal, Itelmen and Koryaks. The pasture has not enough moss for reindeer. Having no reindeer skins, the Itelmen are reported to have used nettle fibre to make ropes and clothing, for the nettles here grow three metres tall, and sting, but they make a good wrapping, and it is said when fish is wrapped in nettle leaves it doesn't rot for ages.

Christina Dodwell, Beyond Siberia, 1993

The rude, wasteful, and imperfect process employed by the natives in preparing the fibre from the manufacture of twine, thread and fishing nets by the mere process of scraping, was wholly inapplicable on a large scale, and besides gave only a very inferior result.

Exhibition of the Works of Industry of All Nations 1851, Vol I

Nettle ethnobotany: the use of nettle fibre by indigenous communities around the world

Wherever a fibre yielding member of the Nettle Family is found there is often a history and tradition of its use for cordage and textiles by local communities. The way the fibre is removed from the plant and the uses to which it is put vary according to the physical structure of the plant, its geographical location and the particular lifestyle and requirements of the communities to whom it is available. The most common species of nettle used in Europe is *Urtica dioica*. Another species, *Urtica cannabina*, grows in Russia and Siberia and is prized for its high fibre content. Where nettle fibre is recorded as being used in this geographical region, it is likely that this is the species referred to. Unfortunately, records of nettle fibre use in particular areas do not always state the exact species, so we have to apply some guesswork according to which plants would have been locally available.

Indigenous communities that populate remote areas of the globe have travelled, intermingled and traded with one another throughout the course of human history. They also shared knowledge of their traditional practices, and similar activities were carried out and transported throughout Russia, Siberia, Japan, Canada and North America.

The earliest written reference we have to nettle fibre is its use in Russia. In 900 AD the Russian Monk Nestorius wrote about wonderful textiles and strong ropes and sails used for boats that were made from nettle fibres.[24] It is generally accepted that during the 9th or 10th century a group of people living on the banks of the River Volga in Russia travelled north-west and settled in Finland in the current region of Karelia. In the past, the lakeside communities living in this area used nettle fibre to make sacks.[25] Similarly the Mordvinians from Central Russia, also of Finno-Ugric descent, are reported to have made sacks from coarse nettle yarn after the Second World War.[26]

Travelling in an easterly direction from the River Volga one will reach the Ural Mountains on the border between Europe and Asia, where the Khanty and Mansi people occupy territory in the Ob river basin. The Mansi men once wore nettlecloth shirts. These garments reached as far as the knee, had a turned down collar and were embroidered with wool on the chest and the hem. During the early part of the 20th century they began to make shirts from cloth they had purchased outside of their region.[27]

The Khanty people traditionally made clothing from hemp and nettle fibre and it is thought likely that this particular weaving tradition had been introduced to them by the Tartars.[28] Their nettle dresses were elaborately embroidered and decorated with glass beads and tin pieces. Both the Khants and Mansis made fishing nets from nettles and later from hemp. They used a variety of bag-shaped nets called *koydon*, primitive dragnets and the *syrp* (a type of two-man seine).[29] Hald describes the method used by these

---

24 Bouché, C. B., Grothe, H., 1884, *Ramie, Rhea, Chinagras und Nesselfaser*, 2. Aufl., Springer, Berlin, pp. 1-156.
25 Hakkarainen, L., 2001, personal communication.
26 Salo, Merja, L. T., 2002 6th February, personal communication.
27 Levin, M., Potapov, L, (eds.), 1964, *The Peoples of Siberia*, University of Chicago Press.
28 Oakes, J., Riewe, R., 1998, *Spirit of Siberia*, Smithsonian Institution Press.
29 Levin and Potapov, 1964

groups to prepare the fibre:

> The nettle plants are thoroughly dried, they are then moistened and split with a knife of pine or bone. The pith is removed from the woody stalks with the teeth, and other useless matter is discarded. The outer fibrous part, the sclerenchyma, is then softened by beating – either with a club or by pestle and mortar. The tow is removed by rubbing the fibre between the hands or with a sort of scraping knife.[30]

Another description of the process records that the nettles were collected in the autumn, the stalks peeled and only the outside fibrous coating kept. This was then carded with a clamshell, bundled up and stored until winter. It was then soaked in water until the connective tissue began to dissolve, before being buried in snow for several weeks until the fibres started to separate. The fibres were then twisted into two-ply thread, netting, multi-ply yarn or rope.[31]

The Bashkirs and Sagai Tartars occupied the southern foothills of the Ural Mountains. These communities also used nettles to make nets and thread for sewing:

> Of the Bashkirs, it is further reported (during the 1870s) that 'larger pieces of linen for clothes they mostly make themselves, also... spinning yarn from the common large nettle.' The nettle grows in the rich soil round the houses and is treated in the autumn like hemp; pulled, dried and soaked. The bast can usually be treated by hand, by a kind of maceration. It is then freed from the wood and is finally pounded in a wooden mortar.[32]

Further references can be found to Eurasian communities using nettle fibre. The Chelkans and Kumandins, belonging to a large group of people known as the Altays who inhabit an area on the southern border of Siberia in the Altay Mountains, once made

30 Hald, 1980
31 Oakes and Riewe, 1998
32 Hald, 1942

their shirts and trousers from homespun hemp or wild nettle. On the eastern side of Siberia, bordering the Pacific Ocean, widely distributed communities used nettle fibre to make fishing nets. These included the Udegeys, Orochi and Ul'chi peoples who lived in the Khabarovsky region alongside the Sea of Japan, as well as the Nivkhis who lived just north east on the lower reaches of the River Amur and the Island of Sakhalin. Fish were an important part of their diet and seines and nets of various sizes and constructions were made from nettle fibre.[33]

Along the Siberian coast of the Sea of Okhotsk, to the north of Japan, the Evens used fishing nets of nettle fibre, as did the Itelmen who lived on the Kamchatka River, between the Sea of Okhotsk and the Bering Sea.[34] These were fishermen who lived in permanent settlements and fished with hooks and nets woven of nettle fibre. The importance of the nettle plant for these fishermen was recorded by Krasheninnikov in 1764:

> Few plants are of more general use than the nettles; for being without any kind of hemp, they would have no materials to make nets for fishing, which is absolutely necessary for the support of life. They pull them up in the months of August or September, and binding them in bunches lay them to dry in the shade. When they dress them, they first split them with their teeth, then peel off the skin, or beat them. After this they comb them, then spin them between their hands, and wind them up upon spindles. The thread of the first spinning they use for sewing, but to make their nets they double and twist it; which, after all, never lasts above one summer. The truth is they are very ignorant and unskilful in this manufacture; and moreover they neither steep

---

33 Levin and Potapov, 1964
34 Arutiunov, S. A., 1998a, 'Even: Reindeer Herders of Eastern Siberia', in *Crossroads of Continents*, W. Fitzhugh and A. Crowell, (eds.), Baltimore, MD Smithsonian Institute Press; Arutiunov, S. A., 'Koryak and Itelmen: Dwellers of the Smoking Coast' in *Crossroads of Continents*, W. Fitzhugh and A. Crowell, (eds.)., Baltimore, MD Smithsonian Institute Press; Levin and Potapov, 1964.

their nettles, nor boil their yarn.[35]

Another source shows that the women spun the thread for the nets and also used it to weave mats and sew clothes.[36] A further detailed account describes how the Kamchatkans pulled the nettles out of the earth in August and September, bound them in a bundle and dried them in an open barn or in the air. The stalks were then split with a knife along their length, the bast stripped off with their teeth and the bundles of fibre swung and hit by a stick before they were spun. An alternative to spinning was to twist the fibres with the flat of the hand. The resulting thread could be rolled into skeins and used for sewing or making fishing nets.[37] An alternative method of combing was to use the wing bone of a cormorant.[38]

Japan in particular has a rich heritage of using many wild plants as a source of fibre, for example, *Boehmeria nivea*, *Laportea cuspidata* and *Urtica thunbergiana*. There is evidence that fibre from the plant *Boehmeria sylvestrii* was used in Japan in approximately 10,000 BC and this traditional practice was carried out until well into the 20th century.[39] When we consider Japanese textiles our immediate thought is of rich silks and beautiful kimonos. These, however, were worn only by the wealthy; most of the population had to depend on other textile sources. From the 15th century onwards cotton became more widely available, but for poor people who did not own land it was necessary to rely on what they could gather in the wild. Wild fibre plants were made full use

35 Krasheninnikov, S., 1764, *History of Kamtschatka and the Kuriliski Islands with Countries Adjacent*, Translated by J. Grieves, Glocester.
36 Levin and Potapov, 1964
37 Bouché and Grothe, 1884.
38 Krasheninnikov, 1764
39 Barber, E. J. W., 1992, *Prehistoric Textiles*, Princeton University Press; Edom, G., 2005, 'The Use of Nettle Fibre in Japan', *The Journal for Weavers, Spinners and Dyers*, Vol 214, pp. 15-18.

of, and because of the effort of gathering and processing the fibre, the resulting fabrics were treasured, re-used and recycled until the end of their lifespan. The tradition of weaving fabric from strips of worn cloth, using a bast fibre warp, was known as *Sakiori*.[40]

What becomes clear when a map of this region is represented on a globe – as opposed to a standard world map – is that it appears to be a mere step across the Bering Strait from the eastern edge of Siberia to the north west coast of the United States and Canada. Mingling and trading between the continents would have taken place quite easily. The indigenous peoples that inhabited many coastal communities on the north west North American continent mirrored the use of nettle fibre found amongst the communities that lived in Siberia and employed many plant and animal species for their technologies to a very high standard. The main use of nettle fibre was as cordage for fishing lines and nets, although further inland a wider range of uses was employed.

The coastal groups who commonly made use of nettle fibre included the Straits Salish, Halkomelem, nearly all the West Washington communities, Squamish, Kwakwaka'wakw (Kwakiutl), Nuu-chah-nulth (Nootka), Nuxalk (Bella Coola), Tsimshian, Haida, Tlingit, Nisga'a (Niska), Gitxsan (Gitskan), Dakelh (Carrier), In-SHUCK-ch (Lower Lillooet) and Nlaka'pamux (Lower Thompson).[41] As with small scale textile production the world over, it was generally the task of women to

---

40 Yoshida, Shin-Ichiro, Williams, Dai, 1994, Riches from Rags, Saki-Ori and Other Recycling Traditions in Japanese Rural Clothing, San Francisco Craft & Folk Art Museum.
41 The names of First Nations communities given in the referenced literature (shown in brackets) have been updated to reflect traditional identifications as opposed to administrative designations.

prepare the fibre.[42]

Several groups lived on what is now Vancouver Island and ethnological records describe methods of processing nettle fibre and its uses. The Salish people dried the nettles over a fire:

> ...The outer skin was cracked off and the fibres separated from the inner pith and spun on the bare thigh or with a wooden disk spindle. The individual strands were spliced together by rolling and twisting. The resulting thread was twisted into a two-or four-ply twine.[43]

The Hesquiaht people cut nettles in late summer and early autumn, and dried, peeled and pounded them with a stone to crush them a little. The bast was then soaked in salt water for a short period of time and the fibre beaten to remove all unwanted pithy material. The Saanich people spun nettle fibre with bird down to make blankets and sleeping bags,[44] while the Nlaka'pamux (Thompson) people from British Columbia used the fibre from *Urtica dioica* as thread.[45] Crossing inland to the United States of America, two main nettle species were used for their fibre properties: *Urtica dioica* and *Laportea Canadensis* (Canadian Wood Nettle). Other species also available in this region were *Urtica holosericea*, *Urtica lyalli*, *Urtica gracilis* and *Urtica serra*.[46]

42 Turner, J., 1979, *Plants in British Columbia Indian Technology*, British Columbia Provincial Museum.
43 Turner, N. J. Thomas, J., Carlson, B. F., Ogilvie, R. T., 1983, 'Ethnobotany of the Nitinaht Indians of Vancouver Island', *Occasional Papers Series*, No. 24, British Columbia Provincial Museum and Parks, Canada.
44 Turner et al, 1983.
45 Turner, N. J., Thompson, L.C., Thompson, M. T., York, A. Z., 1990, *Thompson Ethnobotany*, Royal British Columbia Museum, p.289.
46 Ballard Drooker, P., 1992, *Mississippian Village Textiles at Wickliffe*, The University of Alabama Press; Strike, S. S., 1994, *Ethnobotany of the California Indians, Vol 2: Aboriginal Uses of California's Indigenous Plants,* Champaign, IL: Koeltz Scientific Books, p. 10; Smith, H. H., 1932, 'Ethnobotany of the Ojibwe Indians', *Bulletin of the Public Museum of Milwaukee*, Vol 4, No. 3, pp. 327-525; Smith, H. H., 1933, 'Ethnobotany of the Forest Potawatomi Indians', *Bulletin of the Public Museum of Milwaukee,* Vol. 7, No. 1, pp 1-230; Zigmond, M. L., 1981, *Kawaiisu Ethnobotany*, University of Utah Press, p. 68.

The Menominee of Milwaukee used the nettle *Laportea Canadensis* to make twine and bags, while the Ojibwe from the same region used the same plant as sewing thread. The Omaha women of Nebraska pounded the fibres of one species of nettle until they were soft and pliable, then braided them into strips to make belts and sashes.[47]

If we were to explore indigenous cultures in other parts of the world we would find many more examples of communities using the fibre of locally available species of *Urticaceae* plants. For example, people living in mountainous areas of Nepal who possess little or no land on which to cultivate their crops traditionally use the fibre from the nettle *Girardinia diversifolia* to make cloth for bags, sacks, jackets, porters' headbands and mats. It is possible to buy products made from this fibre that have been exported to many parts of the world.[48]

As already mentioned, *Bohemeria nivea* is cultivated in India and China as a fibre crop. Other less familiar fibre yielding *Urticaceae* plants have been commonly used. For example, *Urera oligoloba* in Madagascar has been used to make bags and cloth, and *Touchardia latifolia* or Olona is used in Hawaii for cordage.[49]

---

47 Paterek, J., 1994, *Encyclopaedia of American Indian Costume*, by arrangement ABC-CLIO.
48 Dunsmore, S., 1993, *Nepalese Textiles, British Museum Press*, London, p.60; Dunsmore, J. R., 1998, *Crafts, Cash and Conservation in Highland Nepal*, Community Development Journal, 133, No. 1, pp. 49-56.
49 Usher, G., 1974, *A Dictionary of Plants Used by Man*, Constable & Co. Ltd.

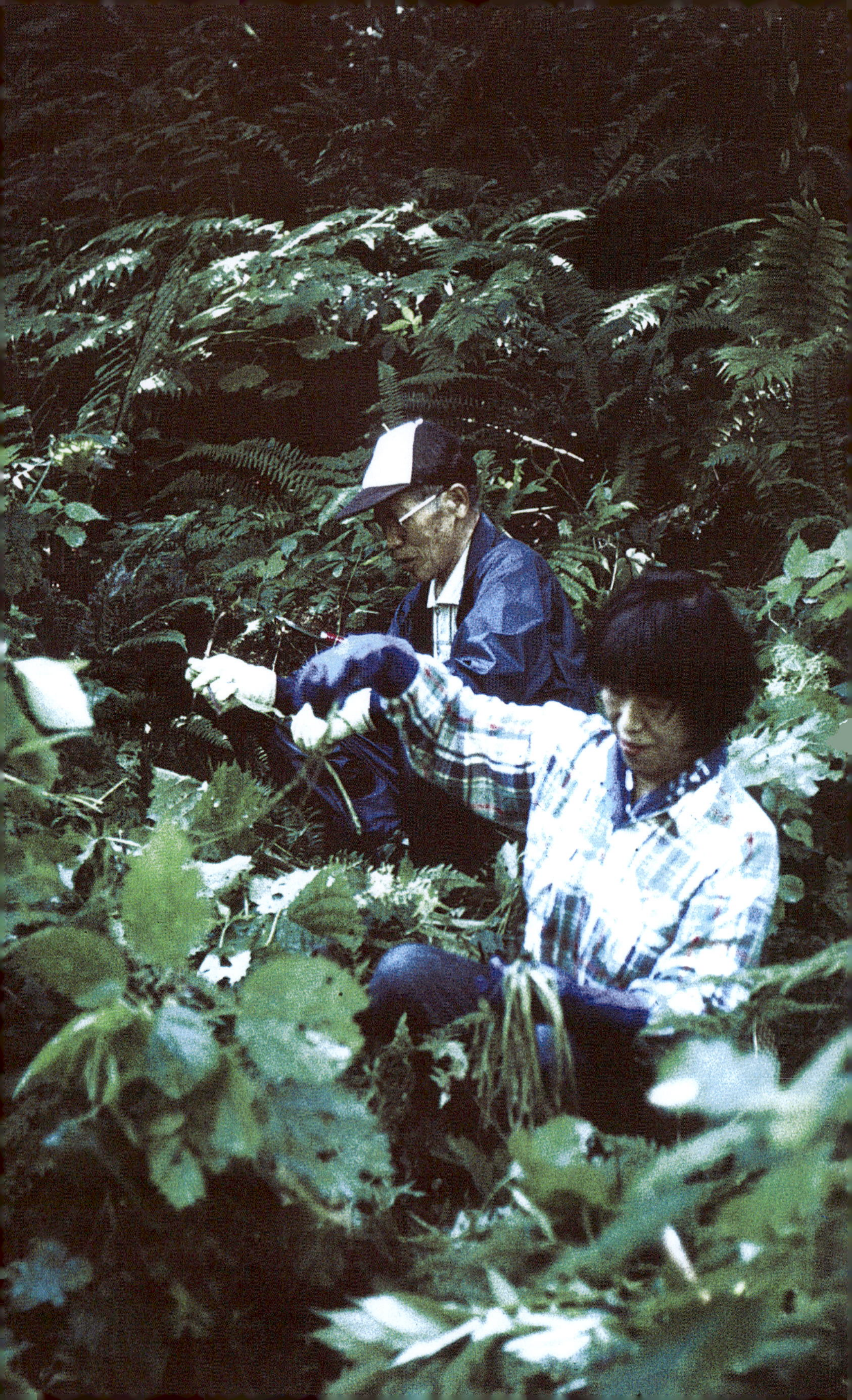

Nettle fibre in Japan

In 2001 I visited Iwate Prefecture in Japan to witness how the wild nettle *Laportea cuspidata* (synonym *Laportea macrostachya*) was traditionally harvested in the Hanamaki Mountains. The traditional use of wild fibre plants in Japan was first brought to my attention by Dai Williams, an expert in rural Japanese clothing.

I made contact with several local people who were familiar with the harvesting and fibre extraction methods and willing to share their knowledge and skills. I was taken into the mountain woodlands by Suruga-San and Harumi Kukita to find the *Laportea* nettle, which was cut, stripped of its bast and the ribbons tied in bundles. Back at Suruga-San's house, the ribbons of bast were soaked in water for a few hours.

Residents from the local village were asked to come and demonstrate how the ribbons of fibre were cleaned. Each strip was stretched out, fibre side down, on a long plank of wood with the root end held securely over the end of the plank. The outer green layer of green plant material was then removed by firmly scraping with a metal scraper. When dried, the remaining lengths of fibre had a similar appearance and feel to raffia.

Fukuda Hare demonstrated how the fibre strips were turned into a workable yarn. The lengths were split with the fingernail into several pieces, then spliced together to make a longer section. A two-ply length of continuous thread was finally spun from these spliced lengths. No retting had taken place at any stage, so the cloth woven from this thread was quite stiff, but with use and washing would soften over time. As with most rural clothing, some of it was dyed with indigo.

The application of these harvesting and extraction methods to the European *Urtica dioica* nettle would be difficult. The *Laportea* nettle grows tall and straight, its bast strips easily away from the plant so it is a relatively simple matter to remove the plant material from the fibre, a more difficult process when applied to the *Urtica dioica*. This means it has been more successful and enduring as a source of fibre for textiles.

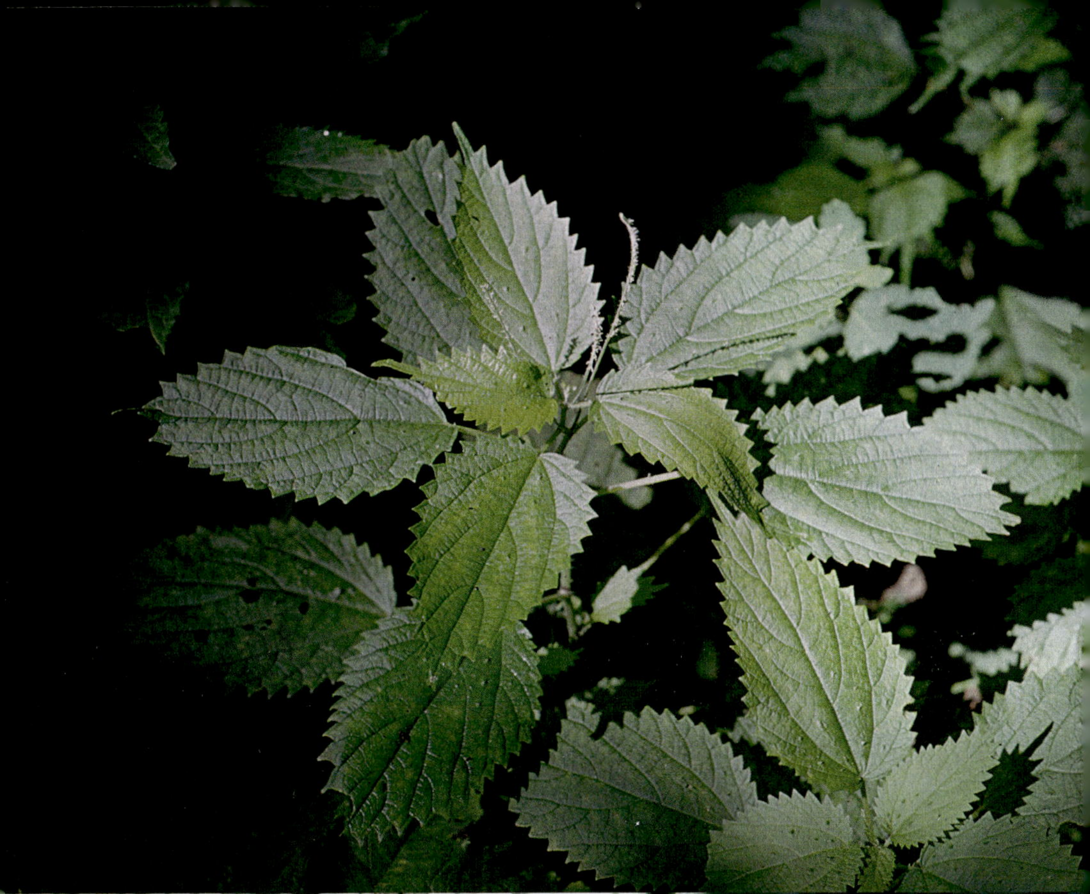

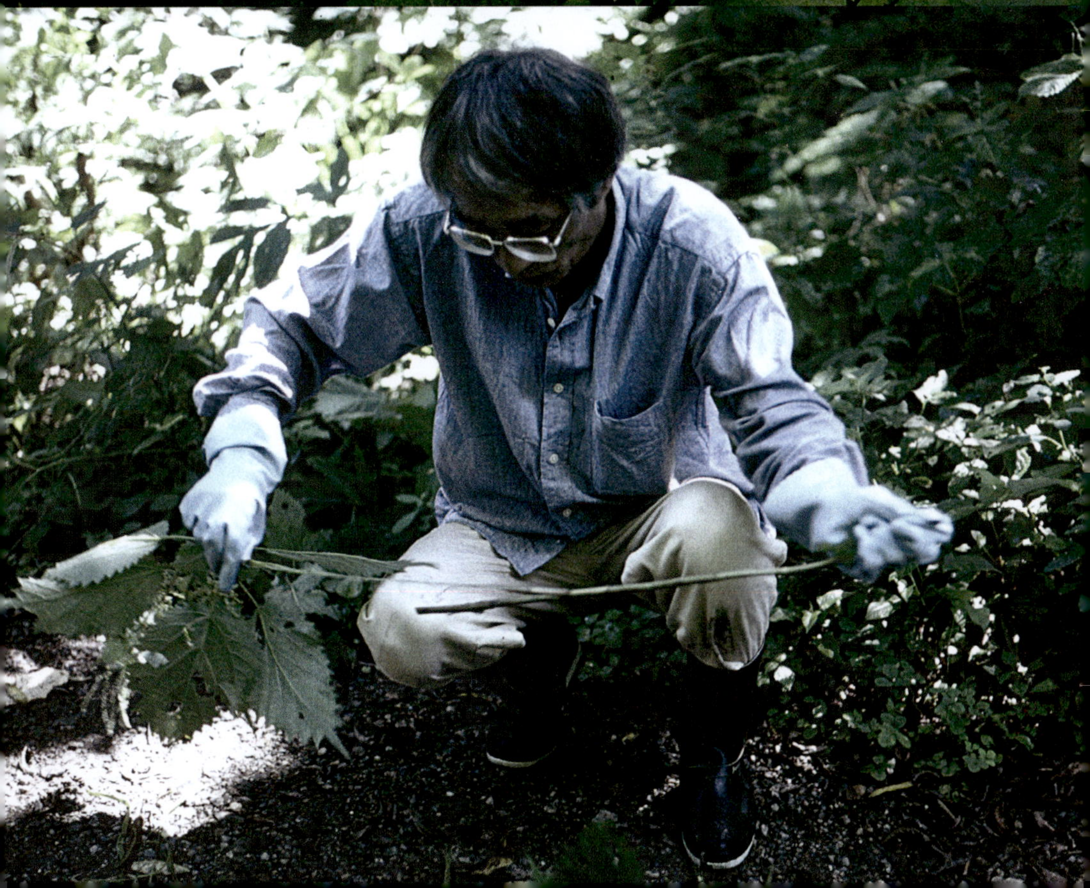

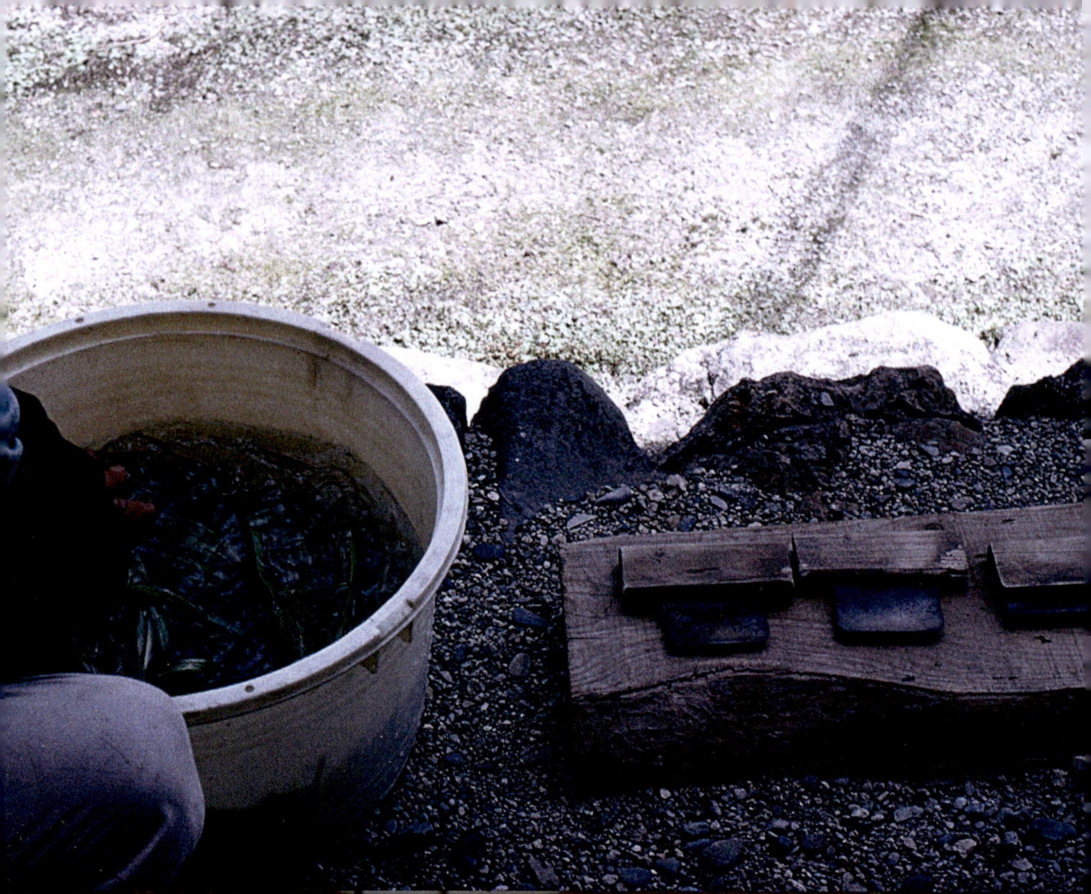

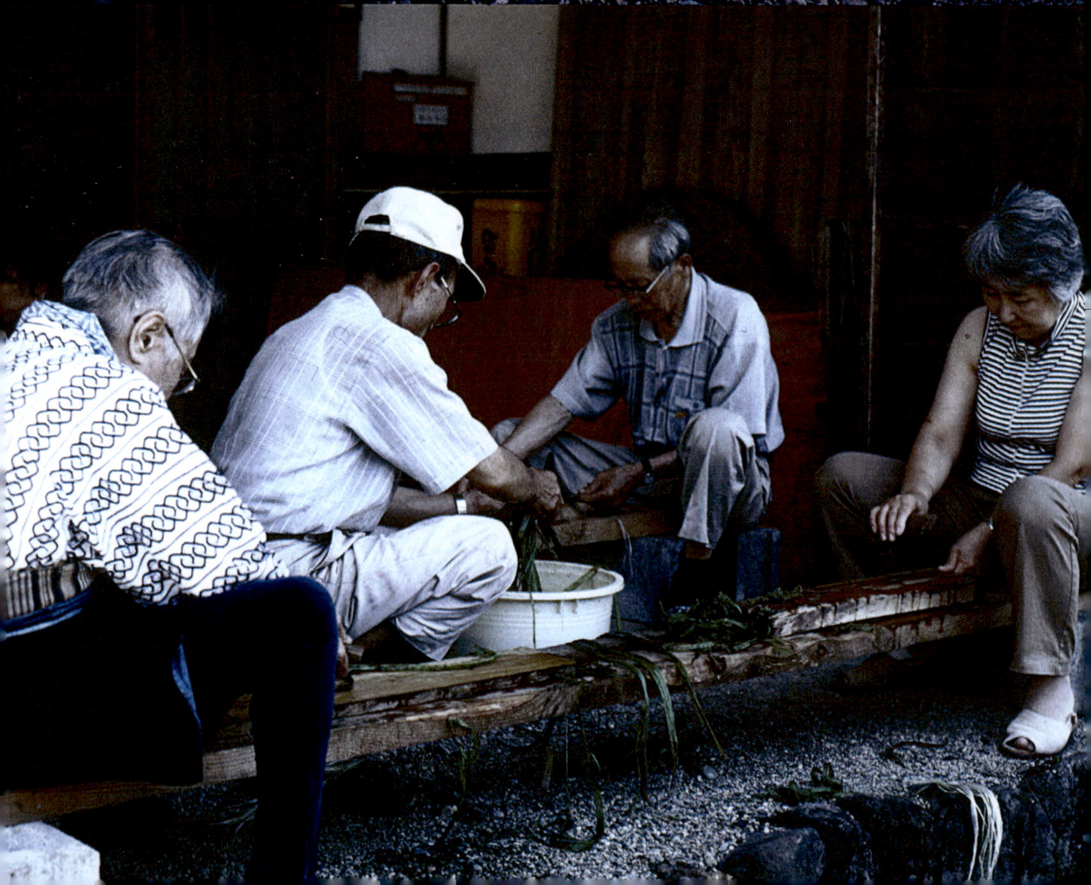

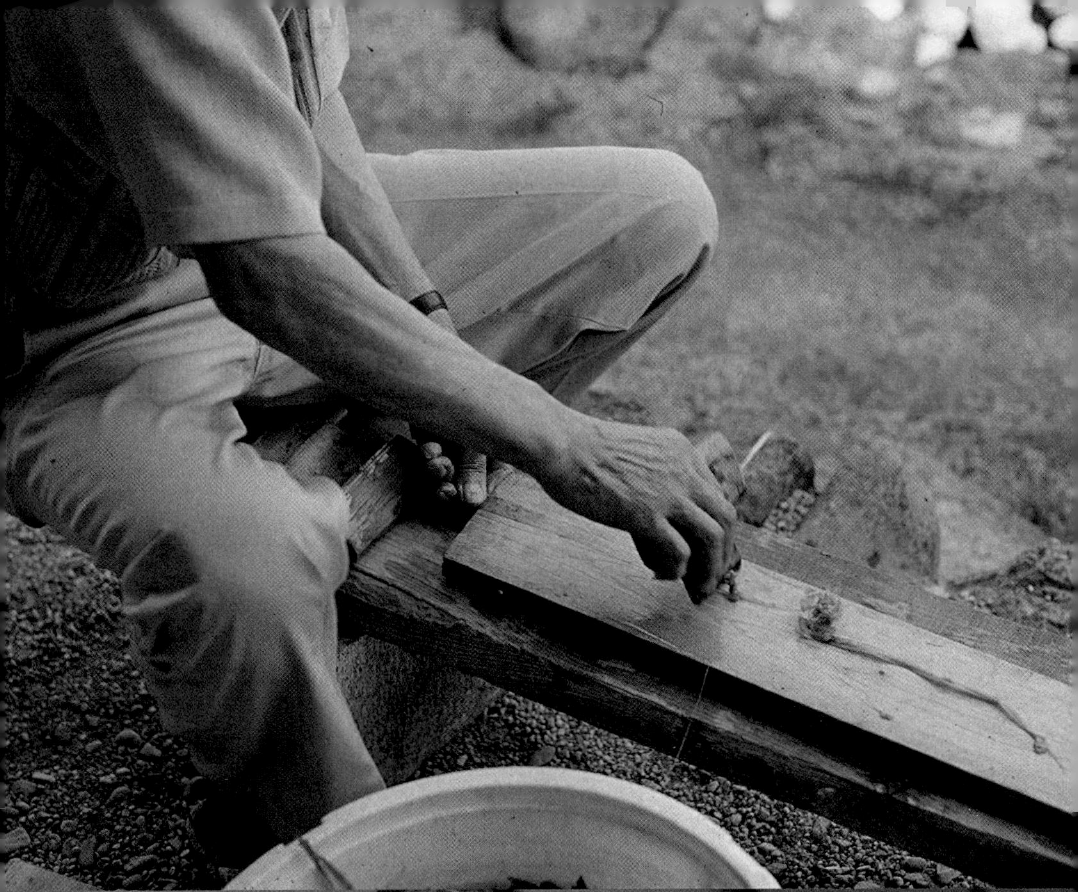
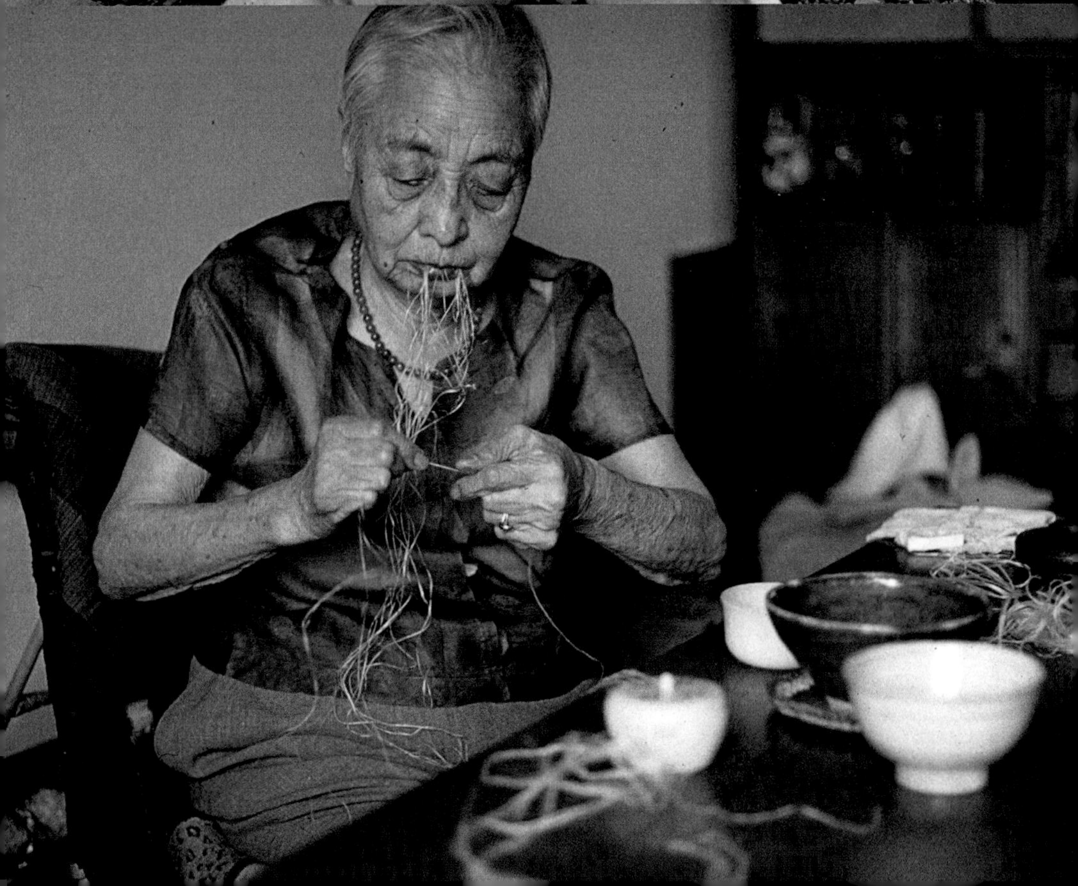

P.48,51: Stems from the nettle *Laportea cuspidata* are harvested in the mountains of Hanamaki in Japan. After cutting, the leaves are immediately removed, the outer bast stripped from the stem, and tied in bundles.

P.52-53: The bundles are soaked in water for a short time. Each strip is then stretched, fibre side down, on a length of wood, with the root end held securely over the end of the plank. The outer green layer of bast is then removed by firmly scraping with a metal tool designed for the purpose.

P.53: The dry strips of fibre cannot be spun so are turned into a workable yarn by splitting the fibre into individual threads using the fingernail and splicing them together to make a continuous length. Fukuda Hare splits and splices the fibres from the nettle *Laportea cuspidata* (synonym *Laportea macrostachya*).

Above, opposite: Samples of textiles produced using the fibre.

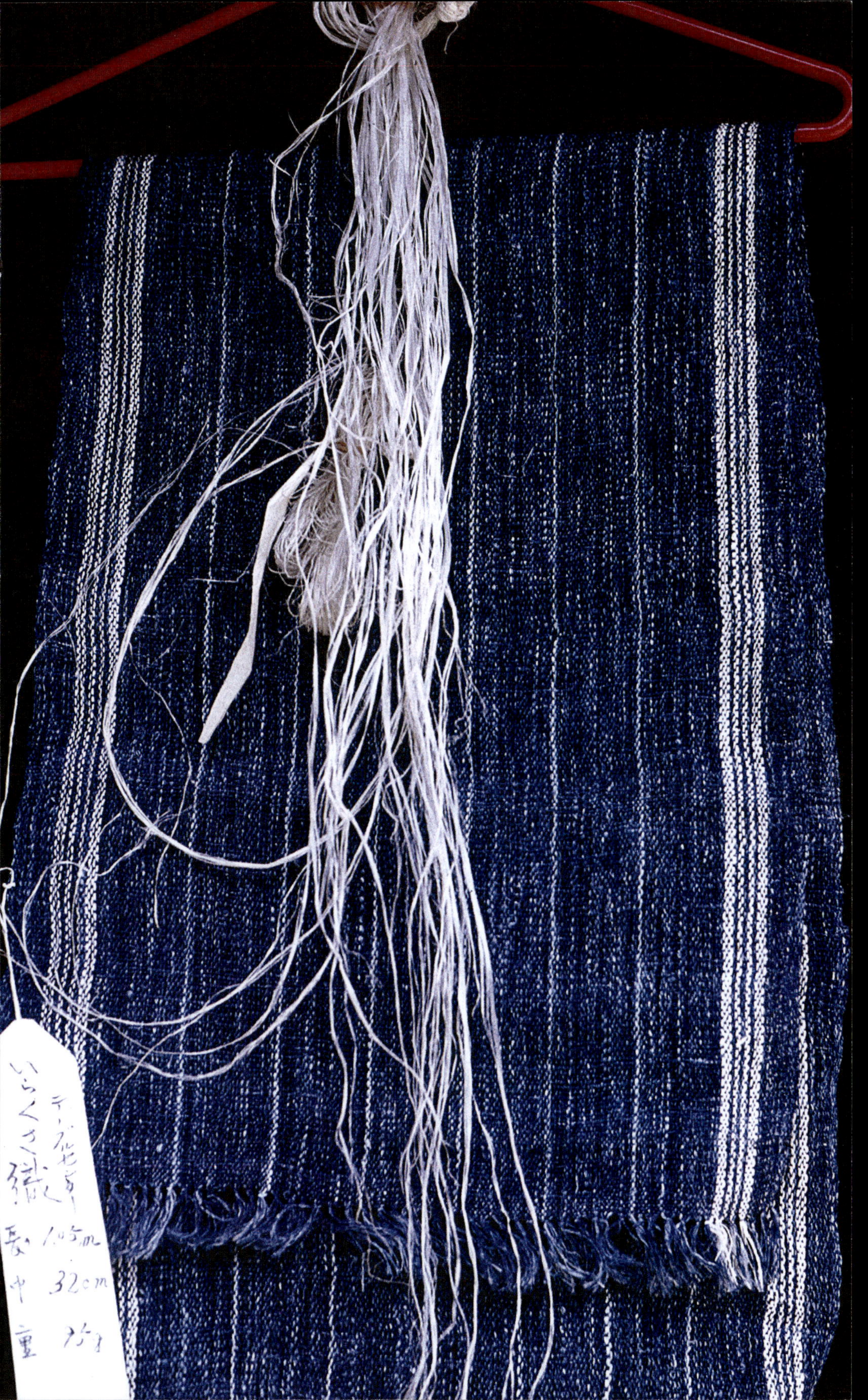

いらくさ織
テーブルセンター
長 1.05m
巾 32cm

One day he saw some country people busily engaged in pulling up nettles; he examined the plants, which were uprooted and already dried, and said:"They are dead. Nevertheless, it would be a good thing to know how to make use of them. When the nettle is young, the leaf makes an excellent vegetable; when it is older, it has filaments and fibres like hemp and flax. Nettle cloth is as good as linen cloth. Chopped up, nettles are good for poultry; pounded, they are good for horned cattle. The seed of the nettle, mixed with fodder, gives gloss to the hair of animals; the root, mixed with salt, produces a beautiful yellow colouring-matter. Moreover, it is an excellent hay, which can be cut twice. And what is required for the nettle? A little soil, no care, no culture. Only the seed falls as it is ripe, and it is difficult to collect it. That is all. With the exercise of a little care, the nettle could be made useful; it is neglected and it becomes hurtful. It is exterminated. How many men resemble the nettle!" He added, after a pause: "Remember this, my friends: there are no such things as bad plants or bad men. There are only bad cultivators."

Victor Hugo, *Les Misérables*, 1862

Early records: the use of nettle fibre in Europe

In the search for further evidence of past nettle fibre use in Western Europe, it is necessary to examine any surviving written records. Sadly these are few and far between, but where they exist should be interpreted with a full understanding of what 'nettlecloth' might imply. The name itself signifies an enduring tradition of using nettle fibre to make cloth. It has been demonstrated that it is possible to produce fine fibres from the stinging nettle (*Urtica dioica*) that have the capacity to be spun into cloth as fine as cotton, although the process is difficult and time consuming. There is evidence that textiles have been produced from nettles for thousands of years, so the name 'nettlecloth' is one that would have been passed down from generation to generation. It is logical that the name would also have been given to the imported cloth made from the foreign nettle ramie (*Boehmeria nivea*). In time, nettlecloth became the term used to describe a variety of textiles possessing the attributes of fineness and softness, a fact confirmed by Bouché and Grothe,[50] who recorded in 1867 that both cotton and linen fabrics were given the name. Even very recently the word *Nessel* was still used on the label of certain fabrics sold in Germany. This does not imply, however, that this fabric contained a single thread from the nettle plant.

Albertus Magnus lived in Germany from 1193-1280 and is considered to be probably the greatest scholar of the Middle-

---

50 Bouché and Grothe, 1884.

Ages. He wrote of the use of the nettle as a spinning plant but observed that the cloth made the skin itch,[51] presumably referring to the nettle *Urtica dioica*, as no other species would have been available if the cloth was made locally. It has often been reported that nettle fibre produces a smooth textured fabric, so his opinion would appear to contradict this. However, depending on the method and efficiency of extracting the fibre from the plant in the first place, it may well have been that Albertus' vest was simply badly made. The complaint that cloth made from nettle fibre is coarse, uncomfortable to wear and caused itching has also been made in more recent times.[52]

Some records can be found in Britain. Latham's *Medieval Latin Word List* links the word *Urtica* with the word nettlecloth and dates this to 1391.[53] The will of E. Careleton, dated 1539, states that her 'best rayle of nettyll cloth' was to be passed on after her death.[54] This could have been an imported textile however.

The use of nettle fibre in the 16th century is mentioned in *The Draper's Dictionary* of 1886:

> A stuff called 'Nettell clothe' appears in an inventory of 1572, priced at 1s the yard. This may have been made of the fibres of nettles, but if so there are many people living who would be glad to acquire yet another art apparently familiar to our forefathers, but which in extensive application, evades the anxious inquirer of our day. Cloth made from nettle fibres has been made in small quantities, but any effort to make large use of them is completely frustrated by a gum contained in the stems, and by the brittleness of the fibres.[55]

51 Magnus, Albertus, *De Vegetabilibus et Plantis*
52 Brøndegaard, V. J., 1979, *Folk og Flora: Dansk Etnobotanik 2*, Rosenkilde og Bagger, Copenhagen.
53 Latham, R. E. (ed), 1965, *Revised Medieval Latin Word List*, Oxford University Press.
54 The National Archives. PROB 11/28 Q3.
55 Beck, Samuel William, 1866, *The Draper's Dictionary: A Manual of Textile Fibres*, The Warehouseman and Drapers' Journal Office, p. 239.

The dictionary entry casts some doubt as to whether the textile mentioned had genuinely been made from the fibres of nettles, and as with Elyn Careleton's will, we should be cautious in assuming the same of the nettle cloth listed in the probate inventory of the goods and chattels of Michael Woodgate of Horsham, West Sussex in 1689. Woodgate was a noteworthy tradesman, and it is almost certain that Horsham was a centre of trade and commerce from its earliest days.[56] It is likely, therefore, that Woodgate would have been favourably placed to buy and sell the choicest of textiles that had been imported from other countries.

The items of nettlecloth listed in the inventory do not seem of great monetary value. We might ask what the quality of the cloth was. Was it flimsy rather than heavy? Could it have been imported under the name nettlecloth but actually been made from some other fibre? By the 19th century 'nettlecloth' had become firmly established as the name for any textile possessing certain characteristics, and also might well have been used to describe fabric made from imported ramie (*Boehmeria nivea*). It also seems to refer to some rather unsuccessful attempts to use the common nettle (*Urtica dioica*) as a source of fibre during that particular period. We can only guess at the truth.

Scotch Cloth

There is no doubt that wherever nettles grow, someone at some point will have extracted fibre from the plants, and Scotland would have been no exception. Scotch Cloth is a fabric that originated in Scotland that may, at least initially, have been made

---

56 Hughes, Annabelle, F., 1999, *Clothyng Oft Maketh Man: Goods and Chattels of some Horsham Tradesmen, 1626-1734*

A true and perfect Inventory of all and
singular the goods Chattells & Creditts of
Margarett Woodgate late of Wrexham in the
County of Suff. Mercer deceased, taken
apprized the Nyne & twentyth day of December
in the yeare of our Lord Christ one thousand
six hundred seaventy & Nyne by John Badly
& Thomas Lutab both of Wrexham aforesaid
as followeth:

           li — s — d

Goods in the Shopp

Impr: 28 Ells ½ of floren Cloth at 16d p Ell —— j — viij — o
It five Ells ¼ of floren Cloth at 1s p Ell ——— o — vj — o
It 30 Ells ¾ of Cambrough Cloth ——————— o — xv — o
Item 7 Ells ¼ of floren Cloth at 7d p Ell ——— iiij — ij — ¼
It twenty yds of white & Coloured Callico —— o — o — o
It 3 yds of Buckerom ——————————————— o — ij — ij
It 10 Ells of Nettle Cloth at 5d p Ell ————— o — iiij — o
It 17 Ells ¾ of floren Cloth ——————————— o — o — o
It 9 Ells of Narrow Cloth ——————————— o — ij — iiij
It 18 Ells of Canvas at 14d ——————————— j — j — o
It 6 Ells of Droyed ——————————————— o — o — o
It 15 yds ½ of narrow Droyed & thin Coneso Cloth
 at 5d p yd ——————————————————— o — vj — o
It 40 yds of blue Linnen narrow ——————— j — o — o
Item 23 yds of broad blue Linnen at 6d p yd — o — xj — viij
It 3 yds of Linsey woolsey blue ——————— o — ij — ij
It 28 yds ½ of Nettle Cloth at 3d p yd ———— o — vij — ob
It 6 yds of Lynnen Linnen 8d p yd ————— o — iiij — iiij
Item 2 fattos ————————————————— o — iiij — o
It 5 yds ½ of broad Cloth at 5d p yd ———— j — vij — vj
It 12 yds of Cofe Cloth in remnants ———— o — iiij — o
It 12 remnants of Linnen Cloth —————— o — vij — o
It 6 yds ½ of ruffled holland ——————— o — vj — vj
It 7 yds of Linnakey ——————————— o — iiij — viij
It 3 remnants of Canvas and Linnen & Sacking — o — iiij — o
It 8 yds of Genting at 18d

Goods in the Shopp	£	s	d
Imps 28 Ells & ½ of Flexen Cloth at 16d P Ell	i	xviii	o
It five Ells & ½ of Flexen Cloth at 2d P Ell	o	xi	o
It 30 Ells & ¾ of Hamborough Cloth	o	xv	o
Item 7 Ells & ¼ of Flexen Cloth at 7d P Ell	o	iiii	ii
IT Twenty yds of white & Coloured Callico	o	x	o
It 3 yds of Buckerom	o	ii	ii
It 10 Ells of Nettlecloth at 3d P Ell	*o*	*iiii*	*o*
It 17 Ells & ¾ Flexen Cloth	o	x	o
It 9 Ells of Narrowe Cloth	o	ii	iii
It 18 Ells of Canvas at 14d	i	i	o
It 6 Ells of Troyes	o	v	o
It 15 yds & ½ of Narrow Troves & other Course Cloth at 5d P yd	o	vi	v
It 40 yds of blue Linnen narrowe	i	o	o
Item 23 yds ¾ of broad blue Linnen at 6d P yd	o	xi	viii
Item 3 yds & ¾ Linsey Woolsey blue	o	ii	vi
It 28 yds & ½ of Nettle Cloth at 3d P yd	*o*	*vii*	*i*
It 6 yds ½ of Dymon Linnan 8d P yd	o	iiii	iiii
Item 2 sackes	o	iiii	o
It 5 yds & ½ of broadcloth at 5s P yd	i	vii	vi

Above: Transcription of the probate inventory of the goods and chattels of Michael Woodgate of Horsham, West Sussex, 1689. My thanks to Annabelle Hughes for bringing this record to my attention.

Opposite: Original document. Will registers, 1678-1688, (MF 191), West Sussex Record Office.

from the fibres of stinging nettles, though there are few records to support the claim.

This one from 1682, recorded by botanist Nehemiah Grew, is probably the best known:

> And scotch-cloth is only the housewifery of (the sap-vessels) of the barque of nettle[sic].[57]

An interesting account appeared in the Dundee Advertiser during the 1800s, recorded by Lady Wilkinson in her book of 1888. It would be fascinating to know more about the history of this piece of fabric:

> I enclose a small piece of cloth, a bit of the flag of the Tailor Incorporation, Arbroath, made in 1670, as recorded in the minute book of the craft, from the common nettle. The cloth, you will notice, is very fragile, a mere rag, in fact – but this may be accounted for by age and exposure to the weather, when the worthy craft celebrated gala days by processions, etc.[58]

Scotch Cloth was a plain quality material that appears to have been made for general household use:

> Scotch cloth… is a sort of white sleasie soft-cloth and since calico had been dear, is much used for linens for beds and window curtains.[59]

It is unlikely that the Scotch Cloth widely mentioned in, for example, 17th century inventories and wills would have actually been made from nettle fibre. There was quite a range of fabrics available for people to buy at the time and these were largely

---

57 Grew, Nehemiah, 1682, *The Anatomy of Plants with an Idea of a Philosophical History of Plants*, Printed by W. Rawlins, for the author, p.13.
58 Wilkinson, Lady Caroline Catharine, 1888, *Weeds and Wild Flowers*, John van Voorst, pp. 1-7.
59 F. J., 1695, *The Merchant's Warehouse Laid Open*, London.

variations of cotton and linen.[60] If the significant quantities of Scotch Cloth also accessible had been made from nettle fibre, then someone somewhere would have had to work extremely hard to produce it. What is notable, in view of this, is the lack of records relating to any significant scale of nettle cultivation and harvest, or subsequent processing of fibre and manufacturing of fabric.

Scotch Cloth is therefore probably another example of a fabric that may once have been made from nettle fibre but was later produced from other fibres. Flax became a widely cultivated plant in Scotland by the beginning of the 18th century and important to the Scottish economy, and many families grew and spun their own. It was then taken to a local weaver to be woven before the resulting material was turned into family and household goods.[61] The practice of using nettle fibre may have continued in Scotland on a small scale, but not enough to leave samples for us to look at today. Scotch Cloth's legacy as a nettle fibre based textile remains in the following famous passage, written by Thomas Campbell while travelling abroad during the early part of the 19th century.

> Last of all, my eye luxuriated in looking on large and beautiful beds of nettles. 'Oh, wretched taste!' your English prejudice perhaps will exclaim: 'is not the nettle a weed if possible more vile than even your Scottish thistle?' But be not nettled my friend, at my praise of this useful weed. In Scotland, I have eaten nettles, I have slept in nettle sheets, and I have dined off a nettle table-cloth. The young and tender nettle is an excellent pot-herb and the stalks of the old nettle are as good as flax for making cloth. I have heard my mother say that she thought nettle-cloth more durable than any other species of linen.[62]

---

60 Spufford, M., 1984, *The Great Reclothing of Rural England: Petty Chapmen and their Wares in the Seventeenth Century*, The Hambledon Press.
61 Tarrant, Naomi, 2000, Personal Communication.
62 Campbell, T., 1837, 'Letters from the South, Volume 1', first published in *New Monthly*, 1835, London, p. 150.

Nettle Fibre in Scandinavia

Many references to the past use of stinging nettle fibre are found in Scandinavian literature. Accounts of the use of nettle fibre textiles exist from the 15th to the 20th centuries. As many of as these are available only in the language of origin, it is impossible to do them justice here, but we can make the most of what has been made available to us, by Margrethe Hald in particular.

In Denmark nettle fibre was considered to be a good quality cloth. Ethnobotanical collections of 1786 record that very good yarn could be made from the stems of the nettle, and the fibres, which are finer than flax, should be treated as hemp. Another record of 1796 from the same collection claims that nettle fibre bleached faster and retained blue and sharp red colours longer than linen fabric.[63] When nettle fibre was mixed with an equal amount of hop fibre this could be woven into very strong sacks.[64] Advice was given as to how the fibres should be extracted from the plant and prepared for spinning. For example, a Danish magazine of 1792 recommended that when the stems became yellow or dark red, they should be dried, retted and treated as hemp.[65]

Swedish botanist and medical doctor Carl Fredrik Hoffberg wrote, in an article published in 1792: 'If the stalks are prepared in the same way as linen and hemp, they can be spun and clothes made thereof'.[66]

The most comprehensive summary of the use of nettle fibre

---

63 Brøndegaard, 1979.
64 Hoffberg, Carl Fredrik, 1792, *Instruction in the Knowledge of the Vegetable Kingdom*, in Anwisning til.
65 Ibid.
66 Ibid.

in Denmark was written Margrethe Hald in her article 'The Nettle as a Culture Plant'.[67] She gives fascinating examples from books, documents and eyewitness accounts of how the common stinging nettle was used to produce textiles in various parts of Europe and particularly Denmark. For example, she quotes from a children's book of natural history published in 1791:

> Nettle-cloth is made of stinging nettles. Yes, children, like hemp and flax the large nettles supply us with fibres of which the finest nettle-cloth can be woven. But as far as I know, no more of it is made anywhere. It is too expensive, besides not wearing well. But here and there lace is said to be made of it still.[68]

Hald also records an account of how, during the Napoleonic Wars of 1807-14, a doctor's wife named Mrs. Figat from Brahetrolleborg wove a substantial amount of fabric either completely or partly of nettle fibre, from which she made stockings, mittens, bed linen and handkerchiefs.[69]

Similarly, a book written in 1802 called *Magic for Women* advises:

> The nettles are collected at the end of August, as well as in September, according as the weather has been damp or dry. When you see the leaves beginning to droop and wither, the stalks turning yellow, and the seed falling out of the pods, the stalks are cut off with a sickle close to the root without damaging the root, which later on every year gives out more fresh stalks. The nettles thus gathered are now spread out in the open air, being left to dry for two days, that the leaves may easily be detached from the stalks. Then you shake them like hemp, tie them into bundles and let them lie for 6 or 7 days, more or less according to the nature of the weather, in running water.
>
> After this shaking they must be allowed to become fairly dry, and lie

---

67 Hald 1942.
68 Raff, G. C., 1791, Naturhistorie for Børn, Copenhagen.
69 Hald 1942.

in a dry place, so as to be handy when wanted for use. The rest of the work consists in the preparation of the long fibres, for which you use the same implements as for hemp, seeing that both plants are very like each other and yield a thread and linen of the same colour and thickness. The advantage of nettle linen is evident, since the plant itself neither needs care or manure, nor any special kind of soil, nor requires the least expense; nor is the farmer hindered in his work by it. The linen made of it will bleach not only whiter but also quicker than hemp linen. A kind of very fine calico may also be made of nettle thread, the chief thing being that the fibres are properly broken so that what is most woolly can be kept by itself.[70]

70 1802, *Magi for fruentimmer*, Copenhagen.

One day Brock the Badger came home with a bundle on his back ... He unrolled the bundle and spread it on the grass. It was a green cloth wover from nettle flax, so finely made it was like linen. It was strong and stout and there was never a sting left in the nettles.

A. Uttley, Sam Pig and Sally, 1942

Fibre found in fairy tales

Traditional tales are important because frequently small details of contemporary daily life are slipped into stories and poetry. These details later increase in significance as the practices in question are lost or forgotten. Folk tales and stories are part of an oral tradition that travelled around Europe, changing shape and detail until fixed versions emerged in print that bore a greater or lesser resemblance to the original.[71]

We are familiar with Hans Christian Andersen's story *The Wild Swans*, one of the most enduring fictional tales concerning the traditional use of nettle fibre. We may be less acquainted with the story of *The Six Swans* collected by The Grimm Brothers and first published in 1812.[72] The two versions differ slightly in detail, but the stories evidently derive from the same source. Margrethe Hald makes some interesting observations about the origin of the Andersen account. She does not believe that the idea of using nettles came from Danish folklore. All the stories she had come across spoke of using thistles, cotton-grass, spiders' webs and similar materials woven into cloth to break the spell. Her opinion was that the story had come from Lithuanian and Hungarian fairy tales of a princess who spun and wove nettle thread shirts to free her brothers. It was quite possible that Andersen had been exposed to the practice of the spinning of nettle thread as a child and this

---

71 Hald 1942.
72 Jacob, G., Grimm, W., *Kinder und Haus-Märchen, Gesammelt durch die Brüder Grimm*. Realschulbuchhandlung, Berlin 1812.

experience may have influenced his own version of the story.

The story of *The Wild Swans* shares some interesting features with other European nettle tales. In Andersen's story Eliza was instructed to gather the nettles (*Urtica dioica*) that grew on the graves in the churchyard. Compare this with the record found in the Swedish Ethnological Archives: an old soldier born at the beginning of the 19th century recounted that a young maiden should pick nettles on a Thursday night from the north side of the graveyard, where outcasts, rogues and those who had committed suicide had been buried. After picking the plants she must not look back as she left the graveyard. She could then ret, break, hackle, spin, weave and sew a shirt for her sweetheart that if worn into battle would make him invulnerable, just as long as he did not lie under oath or commit suicide.[73]

The roaming nature of folklore tales is further illustrated by a story called *The Valley of the Mourg* that is believed to originate from the Black Forest region of Germany. The story tells of an evil Castellan who compels a young peasant girl to weave a wedding shift for herself, and a funeral shroud for him, on the promise that she might marry her fiancé on the day the shroud was finally worn. He no doubt hoped and believed that these two simultaneous events would not take place until well into the future, but was of course wrong and met an early doom! This story was compiled together with others in a collection published by Captain Charles Knox in 1841.[74] An alternative version called *La Fileuse d'Orties* (The Nettle Spinner) is believed to originate in Flanders. The evil

---

[73] Jeppsson, Ingemar, 1971, *Nätteltyg, Kulturen*, pp. 108-110.
[74] Knox, Capt. Charles, Traditions of West Germany. The Black Forest, The Neckar, The Odenwald, The Taunus, The Rhine, and The Moselle, Vol 1, *The Black Forest and its Neighbourhood*, London: Saunders and Otley, 1841.

villain this time is a Count Burchard. The main features of the story are identical to the German account and once again both spinners are directed to pick the nettles that grew on the tombs in the churchyard. The Flanders version was reproduced by the French writer and theatre critic, Charles Deulin.[75] Andrew Lang then included it in his *Red Fairy Book* in 1890.[76]

Can we learn anything about the use of nettle fibre from these narratives? It is not possible to know how far back these legends can be traced before they were written down. All we can infer is that the use of nettle fibre has a long history and the extraction of the fibre was not considered to be particularly easy. The symbolic use of nettles in literature usually represents abandonment, neglect and wilderness; a graveyard is often thrown in for good measure. The nettle thrives in disturbed ground full of phosphate and other nutrients and is beautifully described by Oliver Rackham in his book *The History of the Countryside*:

> The nettles and cow-parsley are a memento mori, for in them is recycled, while awaiting the Last Trump, part of the phosphate of 10,000 skeletons.

Furthermore, the nettles in these ancient stories possess some form of magic, and while it is not possible in this book to make a lengthy investigation into the folklore of the nettle's mystical properties, many people who have succeeded in extracting its fibres would doubtless describe this plant as magical.

---

75 Deulin, Charles, 1874, 'La Fileuse d'orties', *Contes du roi Cambrinus*, Paris: E. Dentu.
76 Lang, A., 1890, 'The Nettle Spinner', *The Red Fairy Book*, Longmans, Green, and Co., London.

The Wild Swans

Hans Christian Andersen's version

Far away there lived a king who had eleven sons and a daughter, Eliza. These children were very happy until the king married a wicked queen who was unkind to them. She sent Eliza into the countryside to live with a peasant and his wife and it did not take her long to make the king believe so many bad things about his sons that he took no more interest in them.

The queen laid a curse on the brothers. "Fly out into the world and look after yourselves. You shall fly about like birds without voices." The brothers were turned into eleven beautiful wild swans that flew out of the palace window and into the woods.

Eliza was to return home when she was an adult, but when the time came and the queen saw how pretty she was, she became angry. She tried to think of a way to make the king dislike his daughter. She rubbed Eliza with walnut juice and matted her hair. When the king saw Eliza he said that she could not possibly be her daughter.

Eliza left the palace to search for her brothers. While walking through the forest she met an old woman who shared a basket of berries with her. Eliza asked the woman if she had ever seen the eleven princes who were her brothers. "No," replied the old woman, "but yesterday I saw eleven swans with gold crowns upon their heads swimming in the stream."

Eliza followed the stream until she reached the sea. As the sun was just about to set Eliza saw eleven wild swans with gold crowns upon their heads flying towards the shore. When the sun was fully set the swans shed their feathers and became eleven handsome princes. Eliza recognised them at once as her brothers. "We brothers fly about as swans when the sun is in the sky," said one, "but when it goes down we regain our human shapes."

"If only I might dream of how to save you!" said Eliza. During her sleep that night a fairy came and spoke to her: "If you only have courage and perseverance your brothers can be released," she said. "Do you see the stinging nettle that I hold in my hand? Many of these grow round the cave in which you sleep, but the only ones that will be of use to you are those that grow upon the graves in a churchyard. You must gather these even though they burn blisters on your hands. Break them into pieces with your hands and feet and they will become flax from which you must spin and weave eleven coats with long sleeves. If these are then thrown over the eleven swans the spell will be broken. There is one thing you must not forget: from the moment you begin your task until it is finished, even though it should occupy years of your life, you must not speak. The first word you utter will pierce through the hearts of your brothers like a deadly dagger. Their lives depend upon your tongue. Remember all I have told you." As she finished speaking she touched Eliza's hand lightly with the nettle and a pain, as of burning fire, awoke her.

Eliza found a small cave in which to work. She began the task of gathering nettles, bruising them with her bare feet and spinning them into thread. Although she wasn't able to speak to them, her brothers recognised that what she was doing was for their sakes. While Eliza was working one day some huntsmen discovered her. One of them was the king, who immediately fell in love with her. The king took her back to his palace to live in great splendour, but Eliza was only happy when a little room that resembled her little cave was created and her nettles put ready for her to work.

Unfortunately Eliza had an enemy: the Archbishop accused her of being a witch and tried to turn the king against her. He discovered her creeping out at night to gather more nettles from the churchyard and persuaded the king to follow her. Sorrowfully, when they saw what she was doing the king was persuaded that the people would judge her as a witch and so Eliza was condemned to be burnt. While she waited in a cart to be taken to the place of execution she continued to make the nettle coats. At the last moment possible, eleven swans flew down and perched upon the cart. Eliza quickly threw the coats over them and the swans were immediately transformed into eleven handsome princes. However, because she had not been able to finish the last sleeve of the last coat, the youngest prince still had a swan's wing in place of his arm.

"Now I may speak!" she exclaimed. "I am innocent!"

"Yes she is innocent," said the eldest brother and told the king all that had happened.

All the church bells rang of themselves and the birds came in great troops, for a marriage procession returned to the castle such as no king had ever seen before.

The strength of the nettle fibre is much greater than that of the linen fibre, and trousers made of it will even puzzle the boy most experienced in trouser tearing.

> I. Schiller, *The Solving of the Problem of the Stinging Nettle*, 1916

But tell me, I say, where do you get these wares
Which are held by all so costly and rare.
Who brings us such stuff to the country hither,
From the hands of the Indian despite water, wind, and weather?
Where do we get nettle-cloth, scarlet and tobin,
Wall hangings, indigo, marten, sable and ermine?
Through me and my trade: at my desk I sit
While all round the world my orders flit
And neither by the sword, force, murder or manslaughter
But my bill and my business they are brought here.

> M. Hald, 'The Nettle as a Culture Plant', 1942

There does not appear to be any evidence to show that nettle fibre was ever utilised on a commercial scale in Great Britain, with the possible exception of a small quantity in a fancy material made up of a mixture of waste and tow from flax, hemp, jute, nettles, hopbine and other fibrous materials.

> F. I. Oakley, 'Nettle Fibre' in *Irish and International Fibres and Fabrics Journal*, September 1942

Attempts to commercialise nettle fibre

The years between 1500 and 1760 are said to have been some of the most important in European textile manufacturing. New and exotic fibres and textiles such as silk, cotton, calico and muslins gradually made their way into Europe and the British Isles from distant countries, with the Dutch and English East India Companies importing Indian cotton goods in large quantities. Concern over the impact of these imports on the home textile trade led to their prohibition in England in 1700, as well as in other European countries at later dates. It is possible that the Danish *Överflödsförordningar* (Sumptuary Laws) of the 18th century, forbidding the common people from wearing nettlecloth, may have referred to imported varieties of nettle fibre, such as ramie (*Boehmeria nivea*).[77] There was certainly a fear that foreign textiles would compete with those produced by local manufacturers[78] and Margrethe Hald describes this unrest in her iconic paper 'The Nettle as a Culture Plant'.[79] It is reported that the stinging nettle (*Urtica dioica*) was used for its fibre in Germany, France and Sweden at the beginning of the 18th century, but this practice gradually disappeared through the increase of foreign imports from the East Indies.

Germany appears to be the first country to have attempted

77 History of Technology, Singer, C., Holmyard, E. J., Hall, A. R., (eds.), 1965, *History of Tech. Vol 111*, Clarendon Press Oxford.
78 Brøndegaard, 1979.
79 Hald, 1942.

to produce fibre from the stinging nettle (*Urtica dioica*) on a commercial scale. It is recorded that from the 1720s, manufacturers in Leipzig collected wild nettles and extracted a flax-like thread with a view to making a large quantity of nettlecloth. The fresh nettle stalks were gathered, withered, crushed and a type of green tow extracted. This was spun like flax and produced a dark green, even and thin thread rather like wool. When the threads were boiled they became whiter, smoother and firmer.[80] This enterprise appears to have had some degree of success and was certainly an inspiration for others to follow in efforts to find an effective method of extracting the fibre from the plant with a view to commercially viable production. Entrepreneurs from other European countries made similar attempts to cultivate local nettles for the large scale production of nettle fibre.[81] For example, it is recorded that the weaving of fibre from local nettles took place in Picardy in France during the 18th century.[82]

Up until the end of the 17th century the manufacture and trade in textiles throughout Europe was on a limited scale. Many households had to depend on work carried out in their homes by individual craftsmen and women and their families. Some households relied solely on what they could produce for themselves, generally from wool or flax. At the beginning of the 18th century the textile industry in Europe began to move away from local cottage and home industries to larger scale manufacturing in workshops and factories. One of the most important events was the growth of the cotton industry and the full impact of this has been well

---

80 Prosper, F. S., 1799, *Über die Kultur und Benutzung der Grossen Nessel*, Prosper; Bouché and Grothe, 1884.
81 Mannering, U., 1995, Oldtidens brændenædeklæde, *Naturens Verden*, p. 161.
82 Bouché and Grothe, 1884.

documented in other places.

At the turn of the 18th century the manufacture of nettle fibre fabric was taken seriously in Denmark. In 1804 an attempt was made to cultivate nettles for this purpose and advice was given by the Germans as to the best method. The enterprise was unsuccessful and the German adviser was eventually sent back to Saxony.[83] However, efforts continued and in 1870 it is written that nettles were gathered in East Jutland in bundles of ten kilograms and sent off to be turned into nettle cloth.[84]

Another plant that gained popularity in Europe during this period of textile fibre experimentation was ramie (*Boehmeria nivea*). This plant grew in the warmer climates of India and China and had certainly been used to make textiles by the Chinese for many years. It seems to have made its first European appearance in Holland in 1733.[85] Throughout the 18th century it is recorded as an import into Europe and attempts were made to grow the plant in Austria and France. The resulting fabric could be described truthfully as nettlecloth because *Boehmeria nivea* is a member of the Nettle Family (*Urticaceae*). This foreign plant fibre seems to have caused mixed reactions and laws were made to ban its import, along with other materials. For example, in Denmark, where the tradition of making *nettleduk* (nettlecloth) was deeply rooted, a deliberate educational policy was created to encourage the use of the indigenous nettle (*Urtica dioica*) as a textile plant, and instructions were provided as to the best method of extracting the fibre from the plant.[86] It was during this period of history

---

83 Brøndegaard, 1979.
84 Ibid.
85 Bouché and Grothe, 1884
86 Mannering 1995.

that the use of the word nettlecloth appears to have broadened to include cloth made of ramie. In addition, a number of references list nettlecloth along with other fabrics that were imported at the same time. We can assume that the word used in these particular contexts does not refer to the home grown nettle, *Urtica dioica*.

> We have statements from several quarters that a great number of the fabrics sold under the name of nettle-cloth had nothing whatever to do with it; the name, it is said, had in the course of time been applied to imitations made of cotton or flax; and already at the close of the 18th century the designation is thought to be very misleading. It would, of course, be very difficult completely to clear up this question now, yet there is the possibility that the imported materials may have been manufactured from other species of nettles than those growing in our country.[87]

The word nettlecloth continued to be used more widely to describe many fine, muslin-like fabrics, but unfortunately with the passing of time, the word has become a relic of history.

The interesting story of Edward Smith

In 1793 Mr. Edward Smith of Brentwood in Essex wondered about the possibility of using the common and prolific stinging nettle (*Urtica dioica*) as a source of commercial textile fibre. He gave the impression that it was not something he had come across before, for he wrote:

> My discovery of the properties of the nettle is original, and arose entirely from my own observations on the apparent (similarities) to hemp and flax, which I remarked they had when growing.[88]

Smith's aspirations were noble. He imagined that if the general use of nettle fibre became successful, then another avenue of

---

87 Hald 1942.
88 1811, Transactions of the Society of Arts, Vol. 28.

employment could be provided for the poorer classes. Presumably the Napoleonic Wars were taking their toll on the country's resources because Smith made particular comment about the general impediment of foreign commerce and the poor supplies of foreign flax and hemp.[89]

In 1803 Edward Smith discovered an announcement in the Chelmsford Chronicle: the Society of Œconomy in Haarlem (Netherlands) were offering prizes for articles on the best species of nettle for the production of fibre, season for harvest and method of preparing the nettles to remove the fibre. Smith decided not to enter the competition, but instead to carry out his own experiments and submit the results to the Society of Arts for the sole benefit of his own country, England. The Society consequently awarded him the Silver Medal and the Silver Isis Medal for 'manufacturing from the fibres of the common nettle, thread, and articles resembling flax, hemp, tow, and cotton'.[90]

The nettle Smith recommended using was the species *Urtica dioica* that could be found growing in the bottom of ditches, amongst briars, or in shaded valleys where the soil was blue clay or a strong loam. He claims to have gathered nettles up to 12 feet high that had stems with a two inch circumference in places, but admitted that the normal expected height would be approximately five and a half feet. He recommended from the beginning of July until the end of August as the best time to cut nettles, although cutting up to the end of October was acceptable. His prescribed method was to briefly dry the stalks, before removing the leaves and branches and retting the bundles of stems in either pond or

89 Ibid.
90 Ibid.

river water for five to eight days.

> When the fibre approaches to a pulp, and will easily separate from the reed, and the reed becomes brittle and assumes a white appearance, that operation is finished.[91]

After the nettle stalks were removed from the water, they should be rinsed, strewn thinly on the grass and turned regularly to bleach the fibre. The fibre was then removed from the stalks by hand or machine, beaten, dressed and then spun.

Smith submitted a number of specimens to the Society. These included fine and coarse fibres, coarse yarn and paper. Unfortunately, he was frustrated with the disappointing results produced by an unreliable manufacturer who had undertaken to process the fibre and so the experiments did not result in any further trials. Interestingly, as of 2001 the pages of the account of Smith's experiments stored in the volumes of the Society's Transactions were still uncut, indicating that his findings were not broadly circulated.

Shortly after Edward Smith's trials, unrelated attempts were being carried out in the United States. Charles Whitlow discovered a species of *Urtica* that Native Americans had used for its fibre. He named the plant *Urtica whitlowii*, but it was later recognised as the species *Urtica gracilis*. In 1814 Whitlow took out a patent on the plant and the State of South Carolina bought it up for an annual fee of $300. At that time textile manufacturers agreed that the fibre of nettle surpassed flax, hemp and cotton.[92]

---

91 Ibid.
92 Bouché and Grothe, 1884.

Ramie or 'China Grass'

Interest in the potential use of ramie fibre for textiles increased during the early 1800s. In 1815 experiments took place in France to grow the plant for commercial use.[93] By 1840 France had its own ramie spinning mills, Leeds in the UK had one and Germany's spinners were also beginning to show an interest.

Britain's status as an empire put the country in a good position to take advantage of fibres imported from the colonies.[94] William Roxburgh was Superintendent of the Calcutta Botanic Gardens and it was he who first experimented with ramie fibres at the beginning of the 19th century. He named the plant *Urtica tenacissima* because he considered it to have some of the strongest fibres he had ever seen and intended to introduce it into Britain as a commercial crop. However, Roxburgh experienced some difficulty in separating the fibres from the plant. Several different methods were tried and samples were sent to England to be tested by experts and manufacturers. *Urtica tenacissima* was subsequently confirmed to be the same species as *Urtica nivea*, now known as *Boehmeria nivea*, which we know to be a nettle species that has a long history of fibre use in warmer climates.

The pinnacle of ramie's fame in the UK was reached when fabric made from its fibres was put on display at London's Great Exhibition in 1851. Three manufacturers of China Grass (Ramie) fibre received prize medals at the Exhibition for the quality of their products. The exhibits were reported to resemble fine white silk or asbestos, some dyed a different colour and some woven

---

93 Murphy, W., S., 1910, *The Textile Industries, Vol 1.*, Gresham Publishing Co.
94 Bouché and Grothe, 1884

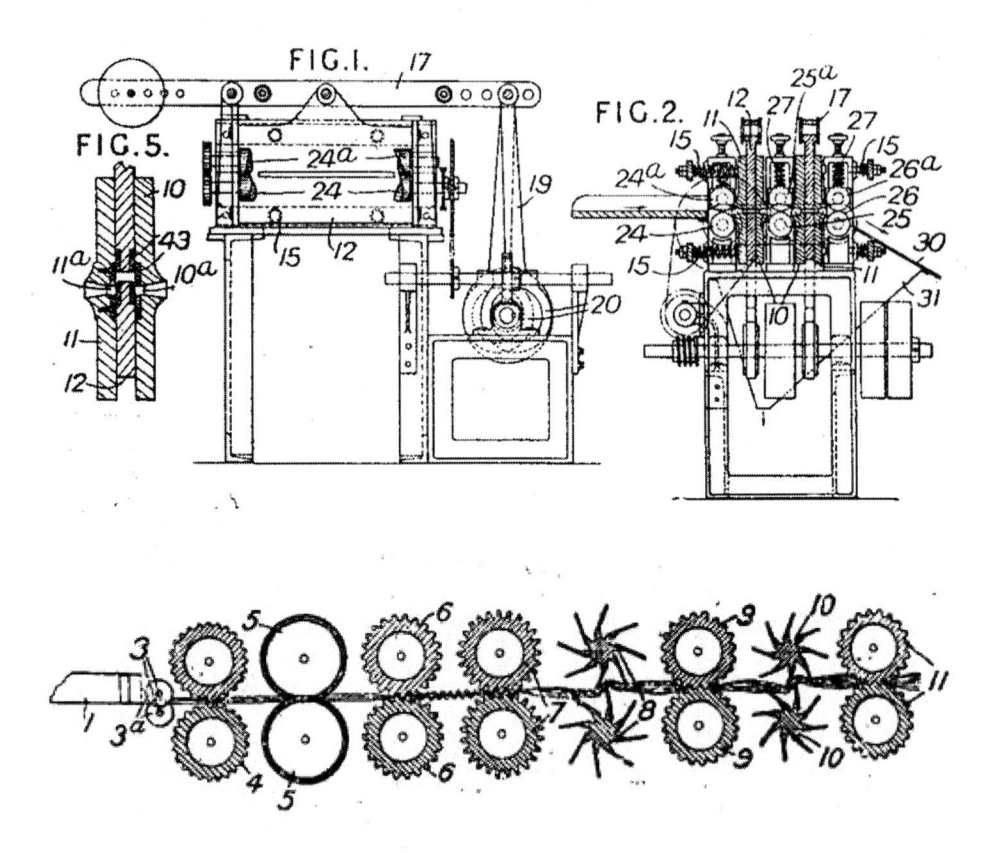

Above, top: Part of a decorticating apparatus patented by G. W. Schlichten in 1919. Schlichten, G. W., 1919, *Means for treating fiber bearing plants*, US1303376A

Above, bottom: 'Machine for decorticating fibrous materials designed by Mr. Ernest Wright'. Wright, E., 1934, *Decorticating Fibrous Materials*, The Patent Office, Patents for Inventions; Abridgements of specifications 380001-400000, Group IX Spinning. Weaving.

Opposite: Leaflet produced by the Nesselanbau Gesellschaft, 1918.

Sammelt Brennesseln!

Bester Ersatz für Baumwolle.

Abnahme und Bezahlung erfolgt durch die Vertrauensmänner, deren Adressen von den städtischen und ländlichen Behörden zu erfragen sind. Wo keine Vertrauensmänner sind, wende man sich an die unterzeichnete gemeinnützige Kriegsgesellschaft, die während des Krieges das alleinige Recht des Ankaufs und der Verwertung hat.

—————— Von dieser sind auch ——————

Merkblätter die alles Wissenswerte über die Sammlung enthalten, kostenfrei zu beziehen.

Für 100 kg trockene Nesselstengel werden Mark 28,— gezahlt!
Für jeden Hektar Anbaufläche werden Mark 400,— vergütet!

Nessel-Anbau-Gesellschaft m. b. H.

Berlin W8, Krausenstr. 17/18 — ab 1. Juli 1918: Mohrenstr. 42/43.

Fernruf: Zentrum 1519, 5958.

into fabric.[95] A method of extracting the fibres used by one of the prize winning companies, Messrs. L. W. Wright & Co., was to steep the stems in cold water for 24 hours then in water at 90°F for 24 hours. The stems were then boiled in an alkaline solution, the fibres washed with pure water and finally subjected to the action of a current of high-pressure steam until almost dry. This method was patented in 1849.[96] After its exhibition at the Crystal Palace, there was great enthusiasm for the potential use of ramie as a source of fibre for textiles. The Government offered prizes for the best method of preparing ramie fibre, and its demand stimulated efforts to establish plantations in a number of climatically suitable countries. Its cultivation was designed as an alternative to the necessity of depending on imports, which by the end of the 19th century were almost exclusively from China.

19th Century Germany

During the years up to 1884, important research into the cultivation of nettles and extraction of the fibre was carried out by botanist Charles D. Bouché and engineer Hermann Grothe. Their aim was to establish the *Urtica dioica* nettle as a true 'culture plant'. Bouché spent more than 25 years breeding the nettle for cultivation. However, after cultivation trials were carried out with the American nettle *Laportea canadensis*, this latter plant was considered preferable in terms of the quantity of its fibre yield. Several methods of extracting the fibre were investigated and it was concluded that most were unsuccessful in producing a clean

---

95 Murphy 1910; Bouché and Grothe, 1884
96 Exhibition of the Works of Industry of All Nations, MDCCCLI, *Reports by the Juries, Vol. 1*, Spicer Brothers, London

end product. Where this was achieved, the fibre itself was often weakened.[97]

Similar experiments and investigations took place in Germany, carried out by a number of different individuals, but it is not possible to say how successful they were. In his book *Die Große Brennessel*, Gustav Bredemann drew from information about nettle cultivation and fibre processing methods from the early nettle history of the 1700s and early 1800s. He observed that it was sometimes difficult for a reader to decide what was true and what was merely propaganda. In his opinion nothing useful about the history of the nettle (*Urtica dioica*) is to be found in the old technological or agricultural literature. What existed seemed to be full of error. His conclusion:

> If someone tried to cultivate nettles in some place at some time, plant history would have recorded it.[98]

---

97 Bouché and Grothe, 1884.
98 Bredemann, G., 1959, *Die Große Brennessel, Urtica dioica L. Forschungen über ihren Anbau zur Fasergewinnung. Mit einem Anhang über ihre Nutzung für Arznei – und Futtermittel sowie technische Zwecke von Dr. K. Garber*, Akademie-Verlag.

As a child at the village school during the early years of the war, we were asked to collect nettles to be made into paper. On one occasion Queen Mary, who was staying at Badminton House, came to visit the village W.I. to see the jam making, etc., that they did for the war effort. We children were lined up with bunches of stinging nettles laid at our feet. Unknown to her, though, they had gone mouldy underneath so were no good at all for the purpose they were picked for.

Violet Spencer, personal communication, 1997

Since the war ended and we have had access to fibres from overseas, all interest in the nettle seems to have subsided. The present high and ever increasing cost of labour in this country makes it seem very improbable that the production of nettle fibre will become a commercial proposition in the immediate future.

Metcalfe, C. R., Archives, Royal Botanical Gardens, Kew, 1940-1946

Where is the nettlecloth today?

It has been shown that records do exist to prove that nettle fibre was used to make textiles in the past. To trace samples of this cloth that might still exist is a different matter. Should they be found, their authenticity must first be established. It is not easy to prove that a particular fibre is from the nettle *Urtica dioica* because of its similarity to other fibres. It is likely, however, that many samples of nettlecloth are hidden away in remote corners of Europe, could they only be found and identified. The following are those that have been preserved in museums and are therefore officially on record.

At the Norsk Folkemuseum in Norway is an antependium (altar hanging) from Glemmen Church, Ostfold. This Flemish weave textile with a warp made partly of nettle fibre thread has been dated to approximately 1700. Most of the weft is of wool, with some parts nettle fibre dyed blue. It has been suggested by paleobotanist, Professor Arbo Høeg that the nettle was probably used a substitute for linen or white wool.[99]

I had the opportunity to examine a very beautiful apron in the National Museum of Denmark. It was finely woven like muslin and covered with an attractive flower motif. The story attached to the apron, presented to the museum for the purpose of identifying the source of its fibre, was that it had originated in the countryside

---

[99] Hoffman, Marta, 1991, *Fra fiber til tøy, Tekstilredskaper og broken av dem I norsk tradisjon*, Landbruksforlaget.

and been made from nettle fibre. If this were the case, then a huge quantity of fibres would have been required, along with the necessary skill in preparing and weaving them into such a beautiful piece of cloth.

There is a fine, commercially-produced cream-coloured piece of linen kept in the same Danish museum that was identified as being of nettle fibre by the Copenhagen Botanical Museum in 1942.[100] It originally belonged to the grandmother of Anna Maria Beata Partsch who was born in 1806 and lived in Adelby Parish near Flensborg. Fensborg is located on the border between Denmark and Germany. This would date the origin of the cloth to the mid to late 18th century and the cloth is thus thought to be a product of the early German nettle industry, likely to have been based in and around the Schleswig Holstein region close to the Danish border.

A sheet originating from St. Viby, Hindsholm, is also included in the collection of textiles at the National Museum of Denmark. The sheet is embroidered at the corner with the initials KND (Karen Nielsdatter) along with the date, 1827. However, the cloth is known to be dated much earlier because it had already been passed down through several generations. As with the previous piece, the Botanical Museum confirmed the fibre as also being from the nettle *Urtica dioica*. It has the appearance of a normal home-woven linen sheet and is well-preserved despite being worn and slightly patched.

Looking at the clues and the evidence for the past use of nettle fibre, a few conclusions may be drawn. The word nettlecloth undoubtedly had its origins in the use of the fibres from *Urtica dioica* throughout various parts of Europe. It does not appear to

---

100 Hald 1942.

have been a particularly successful large scale enterprise, but was probably carried out within the home, in small communities or as a handcraft.[101] To what extent is impossible to say, particularly bearing in mind the confusion caused by the range of fabrics that eventually became known as nettlecloth, a fact confirmed in 1867 by Bouché and Grothe, who said that fabric made from both cotton and linen were labelled as nettlecloth.[102]

The Early 20th Century

Looking back to a more recent period in history, it might have been hoped that the recorded evidence of nettle fibre use would be more frequent and consistent. Unfortunately this is not the case, as war does not appear to be conducive to systematic, well-recorded and careful research. Nettle fibre achieved quite a high profile during the early part of the 20th century and throughout the First World War, but it is still necessary to try to piece together a picture of how and where it was used from what are limited records.

From the end of the 19th century to the beginning of the 20th, the Austrian Professor Dr. Oswald Richter bred a particular variety of *Urtica dioica* nettle known as the Tullner Edelnessel, designed to be cultivated on ground unsuitable for other crops. After experimenting with various methods of extracting the fibre, Richter claimed to have "solved the problem of the stinging nettle." This statement implies that all experiments carried out during the previous 40 or 50 years were not as successful as they might have

---

101 Jessen 1929.
102 Bouché and Grothe, 1884.

been.[103]

Richter's method of fibre extraction was to ret fresh or dried nettle stems in water and then pass them through skinning, breaking and combing machines to produce long spinnable fibres. An alternative method was to 'rot' the stalks, changing the water once during the process, and then boil the fibre in a soap solution. The method described was carried out in ten factories in Bavaria, Silesia and Alsace. These included six rope factories, three jute factories and a cotton spinning mill.[104] It is said, however, that his method was unsuitable for the production of fine spinning stuffs because it did not remove all wood from the fibres.[105] In 1916 Richter predicted that as a result of his experiments Austria would become independent of foreign cotton.[106]

On the basis of these and earlier trials, it was considered a good idea to continue serious research into the use of the stinging nettle as a possible source of fibre, in particular to meet the shortage of available cotton in Austria and Germany during the First World War. One of the economically crippling effects of war are the blocks on imports of raw materials: as of 1913 Germany was importing 447,945 tons of raw cotton, so the onset of war in 1914 required an alternative source of textile fibre.[107]

The perennial problem seemed to be how to acquire enough good quality nettles in order to generate a sufficient quantity of raw fibre. It was of course natural to focus on the collection of wild

---

[103] Schiller, Prof. Dr. I., c1916, *The Solving of the Problem of the Sting-Nettle*, Vienna, Archives: Royal Botanical Gardens, Kew.
[104] 1918, 'A Textile Substitute: Experiment with Nettle Fibre', reprinted from *The Board of Trade Journal and Commercial Gazette*, London, 3/1/1918, pp. 522-272.
[105] Ibid.
[106] Schiller, 1916.
[107] 1918, *Board of Trade Journal and Commercial Gazette*.

nettles and during the war the Austrian Minister of War initiated the collection of nettles throughout Austria and Hungary by school children, soldiers and prisoners of war. The Austrian Nettle Society started with a capital investment of 200,000 Crowns in order to issue propaganda relating to all nettle questions, with the intention of rendering the textile industry entirely independent of foreign raw materials. A similar organisation was also established in Budapest to promote the collection of nettles and stimulate their cultivation.[108]

In Germany the operation was controlled by the *Nesselfaserverwertungs-Gesellschaft* (Society for the Use of Nettle Fibres), the *Nesselanbau-Gesellschaft* (Society for the Cultivation of Nettles) and the *Bayerische Nesselfaser-Gesellschaft* in Munich.[109] In 1915 a total of 1.3 million kilograms of nettles were gathered, with the quantity increasing to 2.7 million in 1916.[110]

Collecting nettle plants from the wild was not the ideal method by which to maintain a constant supply of raw material, in spite of the organised way in which the collection was implemented. Nettles vary in their rate of development according to their genetic strain and the influence of their growing environment. The average amount of fibre in a stem is approximately five and a half percent,[111] requiring the collection of a vast number of nettle stems in order to be able to extract an adequate amount of fibre. The only solution was to cultivate the plant to ensure greater consistency of growth and the consequent availability of a larger number of

---

108 1917, *Der Tropenpflanzer*, pp. 476 & 151, Berlin.
109 Metcalfe, Dr. C. R., 1942, 'Economic Value of the Common Stinging Nettle', *Nature*, 19/7/42, p. 83.
110 Murphy, 1910.
111 Edom, G., 2006, *Extraction and Evaluation of Nettle (*Urtica dioica*) Fibre for Textile End Uses*, MPhil Thesis, De Montfort University, Leicester.

nettles on one site. A place that appeared to be ideal for cultivating the wild nettle (*Urtica dioica*) was identified in Austria, an area of ten million acres located in the Niederwald that at the time was not being used for any other purpose.[112] Richter was sure that ten million kilograms could be harvested in 1916.[113] By 1919 the Germans also claimed to have cultivated nettles successfully on several plantations in Zehlendorf and Nauen.[114] At the Zehlendorf site near Berlin, the residents are reported to have grown nettles of an exceptional size in mud excavated from the Teltow Canal and one year's harvest produced two trucks of dried stems that fetched 800 marks.[115] Apparent progress was made by both Austria and Germany in the cultivation of nettles for fibre, but they were to a large extent in competition with one another and Austria had the edge. This was due to having the damp woods of the Danube Basin at its disposal, an ideal habitat for the growth of nettles.[116]

Professor Richter is reported to have demonstrated his success in extracting the fibre from the stinging nettle (*Urtica dioica*) with samples of yarn and a pair of knitted socks.[117] In anticipation of the possible ways in which the fibre could be put to use, it was estimated that four kilograms of dried stalks were enough to make a soldier's shirt. In wartime it was the policy to gather all textiles belonging to the enemy from the battlefield and subject them to identification tests in British laboratories. Even though fibre from

---

112 1917, 'Successful Use of Nettle Fibers in Clothmaking', *US Commerce Reports*, 8/1/17, p.8.
113 Richter, Prof. Dr. O., 1916, Beiträge Zur Lösung des Nesselproblems, Chemiker Zeitung, p.8.
114 1919, Nettle Growing for Textile Manufacture, *Journal of the Royal Society of Arts*, 8/3/18, p.287.
115 *Der Tropenpflanzer*, 1917.
116 Metcalfe, C. R., Archives, Royal Botanical Gardens, Kew.
117 1916, *US Commerce Reports*, 14/4/16, op.cit.

the nettle *Urtica dioica* may have been used in sandbags and cap and coat linings, the official opinion was that the results were not good enough to consider the serious use of the fibre from this plant over and above other plants that were easier to handle and process.[118] It is frequently quoted that in 1917 two captured German overalls marked 1915 and 1916 were found to be woven of 85 percent stinging nettle fibre and 15 percent ramie fibre.[119] Unfortunately, there do not appear to be any remaining examples of textiles from the First World War that can be proved to have been made of nettle fibre of any species.[120] We are left wondering whether perhaps the original claims were exaggerated, rumours got out of hand or were reported merely for the purpose of propaganda. It is certainly a matter of record that the cultivation of nettles for fibre production in Austria and Germany was maintained purely through vigorous propaganda and that interest died down after 1918.[121] Great claims were made throughout the whole period of the war as to what could be achieved, though there is little remaining evidence that these ambitious goals were ever accomplished. Even within Germany itself there were some who doubted the future of nettle fibre. One German agricultural adviser stated: "The cost of production rules it out for purposes of cultivation, and will stand in the way of its general adoption".[122]

So what happened to the nettle fibre industry when the war

---

118 1918, The Development of the Textile Industries, *Journal of the Royal Society of Arts*, 8/3/18, p.287.
119 Grieve, Mrs. M., 1931, *A Modern Herbal*, Jonathon Cape, London, pp. 574-579; 1933, *Memorandum*, 19/9/33, Archives, Royal Botanical Gardens, Kew.
120 Dreyer, Dr. J., 1999, Personal Communication.
121 von Wiesner, J., 1921, *Die Rohstoffe des Pflanzenreiches*, Wilh. Engelmann, Leipzig, pp. 547-576.
122 1918, *BOT Journal and Commercial Gazette*.

came to an end? While the war persisted and shortages of raw materials remained a problem, the motivation to find a method of producing nettle fibre continued. The Nettle Cultivation Company that had been formed in Germany as a public utility undertaking was anticipated to continue as a profit-making enterprise during peacetime. By 1919 the company owned 28,000 hectares of land, including the plantations in Zehlendorf and Nauen. Its future appeared bright.[123] Unfortunately, the period of research into the potential uses of nettle fibre had been relatively short and theories had not been properly tested. Progress was hampered by a lack of knowledge about the best cultivation methods and how to maintain a supply of high-fibre nettles, the difficulties of extracting and processing the fibre, inflation and the reintroduction of imports of cotton.[124] However, there were fortunately some individuals in Germany whose curiosity and interest in the use of nettle fibre meant that research continued there right up to, during and after the Second World War.

While Austria and Germany were enjoying some modest success with their nettle production during the early years of the 20th century, other European countries were also carrying out their own experiments.

In 1910 H. Grove, His Majesty's Consul in Moscow, reported that a large manufacturer of cotton goods in the district had succeeded in producing ordinary nettle fibre from the *Urtica dioica* plant as a substitute for flax. The method of extracting the fibre was by machine and "the yarn obtained is fine and of very

---

[123] 1919, Nettle Growing for Textile Manufacture, *Journal of the Royal Society of Arts*, January 24th 1919, p.146.
[124] Bredemann, 1959.

good quality, and dyes and bleaches excellently."[125]

By 1917 Mrs. Elna Fensmark of Denmark had the idea of extracting fibre from nettles to meet the shortage of raw fibre brought about by the war. The state granted 10,000 Kroner to carry out experiments under the supervision of a 'Nettle Committee' and guided by the advice of a large number of experts.[126] An example of nettle fibre textile made during this period is currently held by the National Museum of Denmark. This sample was produced by Emilie Backhaus, later Emilie Bjufstrøm. It feels quite rough to the touch and there are still tiny pieces of stem material attached to the fibre, which continue to fall away when the cloth is handled. The documents attached to the sample record that Emilie carded, but did not hackle the fibres. In spite of the lack of 'fineness' of the sample, Emilie made an excellent attempt and I would have liked to congratulate her.

During this phase of experimentation, Denmark's nettles were reserved not only for textiles, but also as a food source for pigs and fowl. 20,000 kilograms of dried wild nettle stems were enthusiastically collected by the Boy Scouts, Boys' Voluntary Band and other groups. A rettery was set up not far from Copenhagen for the purpose of extracting the fibre from the nettles, and a processing method carried out that was quite different to that taking place in Germany and Austria during the same period. The method depended entirely on retting the stalks by means of bacterial activity in a lake or hot water. Unfortunately the rettery was a disaster due to the wrong bacterial cultures forming and creating an 'intolerable stench'. The experiment was largely rescued by the Biotechnical

---

125 1910, Yarns and Textiles: Russia, *Board of Trade Journal*, 10/6., p. 654.
126 Hald, 1942.

Karen Nielsdater's nettle fibre sheet.

Laboratory of the Royal Technical College, who managed to cultivate the 'right sort' of bacteria and so some success was finally achieved.[127]

After the war came an inevitable decline in the use of nettles as a source of fibre as a result of the reintroduction of imports, though the Nettle Committee continued to operate until 1926.

127 Ibid.

After the First World War

The investigations that took place during the First World War stimulated the idea of producing nettle fibre on a large scale – an ambition that did not come to fruition at the time. However, the mistakes and successes of this period were to lay the foundations for greater progress in the years to come, particularly in Germany.

One of the true believers in the future of nettle fibre was factory owner Johannes Elster. In 1920 he described a decorticating machine he had developed, in cooperation with the company Gebruder Uebel in Adorf in Vogtland that could effectively extract the fibre from nettle stems.[128] He was careful to point out that the amount of thread produced was dependent on the plant's growth and harvesting conditions, the method of processing and the intrinsic quantity of fibre in each stem. For this reason he was enthusiastic about the pioneering work being carried out in Hamburg by agronomist and botanist Gustav Bredemann, whose research into nettle fibre spanned more than 30 years, and who attempted to crossbreed *Urtica dioica* nettles in order to produce a high fibre clone. Elster recognised that this was a new era for nettle fibre and he was keen for extraction methods to emerge from the research stage as soon as possible in order to become commercially viable.

Soon after the war Dr Gustav Bredemann started his research into nettle fibre, which continued until 1950. During this period between the two World Wars Bredemann claimed to have bred a nettle containing up to 12 percent of fibre in the stem.[129] The

---

128 Elster, J., 1920, *Referat über die Erfahrungen in der Gewinnung der Brennesselfasser und ihre Spinnbarkeit*, Druk August Geilsdorf, Adorf I Vogtland.
129 Dreyer, J., 1999, *Die Fasernessesel as nachwachsender Rohstoff*, Verlag Dr. Kova, Hamburg.

cultivation of a high fibre species of nettle increased the possibility of processing the fibre more consistently and of maximising the quality and quantity of the final product. He selected and crossbred *Urtica dioica* plants to produce high fibre varieties called 'Fibre Nettle'. The selection criteria were that they should be frost resistant, have long, straight stems with minimal branching and contain a high percentage of fibre in the stems. This very significant research is well documented in Bredemann's book, *Die Grosse Brennessel*, which is illustrated with photographs of nettle cultivation and harvesting.[130] Samples of his textiles made from nettle fibre can still be see in the Museum of the Institute of Applied Botany in Hamburg.

The Second World War once again triggered shortages of imported raw materials. News of Germany's success in using nettle fibre in place of cotton reached England. On the 8th June 1942 The Daily Express reported from Stockholm that approximately five thousand railway carriage loads of nettles would be collected in Hungary during the summer for use as raw material to make textiles in Germany.[131] The Ministry of Supply had ordered the collection of local nettles by the Hungarian population.[132] It was estimated that by September 1942, textiles would have been made from the first consignment and that nettles would be used to meet twelve percent of fibre requirements.[133]

From the beginning of the war onwards, the German Government appealed to the public to collect nettles for use as

---

130 Bredemann, 1959.
131 Metcalfe, 1942.
132 1941-42, *Irish and International Fibres and Fabrics Journal*, Vol 7., No. 5 to Vol 9, No.2, Belfast.
133 1939, *Jute Abstracts*, 30/9/1939, p.235.

a raw material for fibre extraction.[134] This appeal is somewhat surprising in view of the fact that Bredemann had already successfully crossbred and cultivated high-fibre nettle varieties. A United States Department of Agriculture official, who visited Germany after the war to see how the nettle extraction had taken place, was unsuccessful in viewing the process; the one factory that had apparently been responsible for the work was now situated in the Russian zone where he was not permitted access. Nevertheless, he received the impression that nettle fibre had not been used on a large scale, even in Germany.[135]

Bredemann invested a large part of his working life in researching the potential of nettle fibre for textile use. Sadly the old story repeated itself when more prosperous times returned; enthusiasm about the possibilities of nettle fibre use soon waned. By the time his book was published in 1959, any interest had evaporated.

Restrictions on the import of raw materials had a huge impact on Britain during the Second World War, including a crucial shortage of materials to make paper. Throughout that period the World's Paper Trade Review reported the extraordinary lengths to which people went in order to meet this shortfall, including the processing of esparto grass, being encouraged to recycle even the smallest pieces of string and, of course, the use of nettles as a source of fibre for paper.[136] One of the primary purposes for investigating the potential of nettle fibre was to make a strong and high grade paper for 'special war purposes'. It was intended that this paper

---

134 Ibid.
135 Ref. No. 5/N/2/M, Archives, Royal Botanical Gardens, Kew.
136 1942, *The Word's Trade Paper Review,* April 24th, May 1st, May 5th, May 8th, August 14th, September 11th.

be used as a replacement for aluminium in the manufacture of aircraft.[137] Unfortunately the project was labelled unsuccessful predominately due to the logistical problems of gathering enough raw material and the lack of an effective fibre extraction process. In 1962 Dr. C. R. Metcalfe, who led the project, attached a note to the project paperwork which read, "This is a record of the Monument of Folly", and ordered that the paperwork be destroyed. Thankfully, this did not happen and the records still exist as a tribute to his efforts against the odds, along with examples of very fine quality paper and yarn, produced as a result of experiments carried out during the project. These are archived at the Royal Botanical Gardens, Kew, and we should be grateful that they still survive for us to read and learn from this fascinating chapter in the history of nettle fibre use.

137 Milne, R., Hastings, L., 1998, *Home-spun Solutions*, KEW, Spring, PP. 10-11.

Properly prepared nettle fibre is soft, silky and strong, as it would have to be to make shirts. It is not too difficult to produce a thread which is coarse and rough, which weaves up into something like a pan scrubber or a door mat. But to produce the soft, fine thread in any useable quantity – that would be worth knowing.

Beswick, T., 1997, Letter to Editor, The Journal of Weavers, Spinners and Dyers, 147, p.25

A future for nettle fibre?

It is not possible to provide a complete picture of the historic use of nettle fibre. We have only a few pieces of the puzzle, but these are sufficient to show that the fibres from many plants in the Nettle Family have been used worldwide throughout the entire course of human history. The use of the stinging nettle (*Urtica dioica*) for fibre in Europe was not a custom formally recorded by people living busy lives and coping with hardships with which we are unfamiliar today. Our knowledge is gleaned from rumours and whispers of nettle fibre use that have been passed on as hearsay through the generations, along with the occasional written record. Only a very few examples of nettle fibre textiles have survived intact as evidence of this former practice. This is probably because economic hardship made it necessary to maximise the use of all fabrics until they were no longer serviceable. For some people the need to resort to the use of the local stinging nettle as a source of fibre, due to poverty and shortages, created a sense of shame. During the 19th and 20th centuries there was increasing written evidence of widespread efforts to develop methods for extracting nettle fibre, but it is not possible to know the true scope of their success. Claims are likely to be exaggerated, particularly when national governments take an interest. During wartime, or in situations of international competition for resources and technological advancement, propaganda is used as a tactical tool to magnify or invent successes. However, the practical evidence of actual nettle yarns and textiles are still conspicuous by their absence.

Recent improvements in technology and understanding of the best methods for cultivating *Urtica dioica* nettles and processing the fibre have not as yet given the world a thriving nettle fibre industry. This is unfortunate in a context where there is an increasing awareness about the negative impact of the massive polluting and water-thirsty cotton industry upon which we currently rely, and its unsustainability for the indefinite future. Since the beginning of the 1990s there have been attempts to reintroduce the stinging nettle (*Urtica dioica*) as a potential fibre source for commercial textile production. The Fasernessel (*Urtica dioica L. convar. fibra*) has been reinstated and cultivated, methods of fibre extraction and processing have been tested and yet investigative projects have ended, and companies have given up or fallen by the wayside. Only a few remain standing. Why should this be? Is it due to a lack of shared knowledge between the various institutions and organisations beavering away to extract and use the fibre? Or perhaps it is down to the nettle's lack of homogeneity and obstinate refusal to bow to the demands of mass production?

Success in extracting the fibre from stinging nettles has been achieved to a greater degree by individual craftspeople, who have developed various methods of processing the stems and preparing the fibre, although a technique to produce nettle fibre on an industrial scale has had much less success. There are many approaches possible and this has the positive effect of many different methods emerging as a result of individual explorations that make use of whatever resources are available. What is significant is that the opportunity now exists to share skills and knowledge on a global scale, and knowledge sharing communities are beginning to emerge, often amongst those unconcerned by academic reputation or making a profit, but rather for the love of the hand-crafted and – of course – the nettle itself, which has so much intrinsic value. It requires time and effort to produce anything that could be described as a high quality textile. However, anyone may experiment, drawing upon the experience of our ancestors and other like-minded individuals, in order to prise the lovely fibre from the much maligned stinging nettle in their own back gardens.

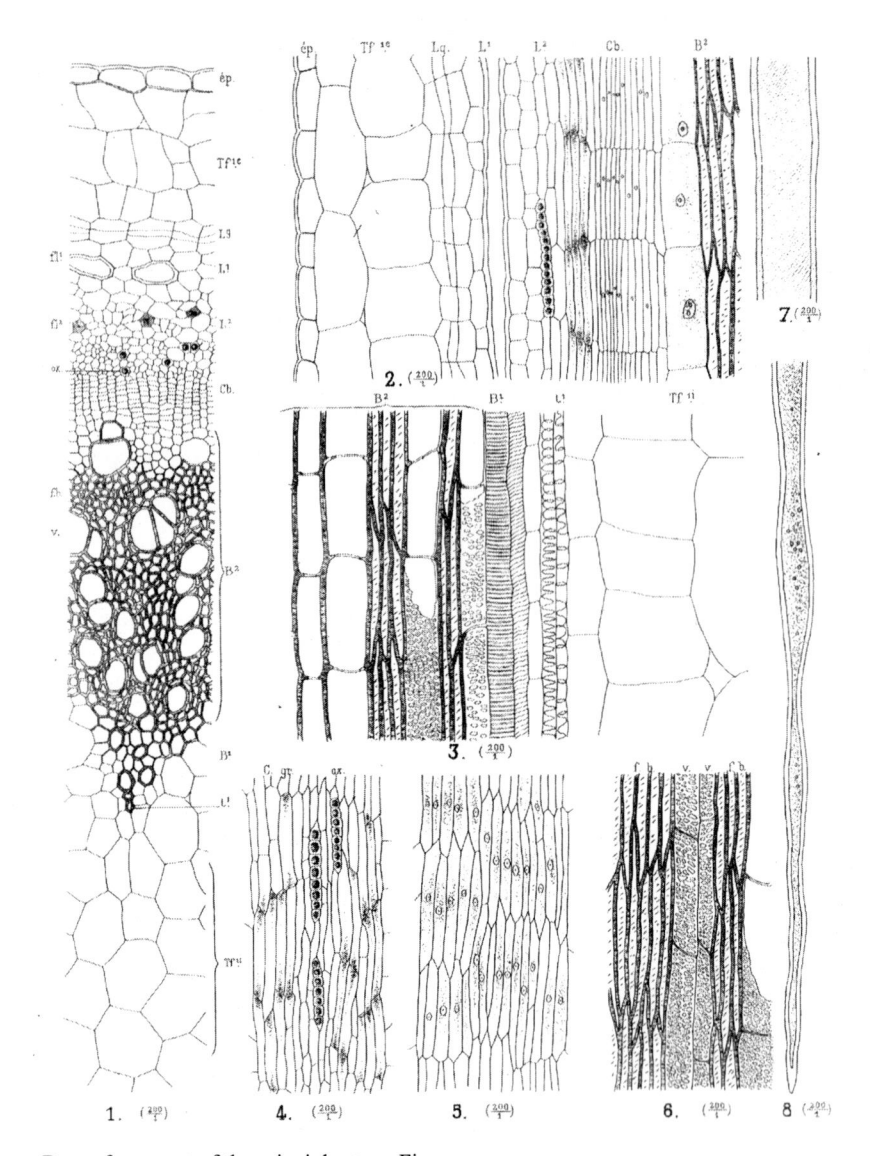

Base of segment of the principle stem. Figures:
1. Part of a transversal section showing primary and secondary fibre production.
2. Radial section through the middle of a stem.
3. Follows previous section.
4. Tangential section through the secondary bast.
5. Tangential section through the cambium.
6. Tangential section through the secondary woody stalk.
7. Middle region of a primary bast fibre.
8. End region of primary bast fibre.

Illustration from Gravis, A., 1885, *Recherches Anatomiques Sur Les Organes Végétatifs De L'urtica Dioica*, L., Librairie Médicale & Scientifique de A. Manceaux, Brussels.

A basic guide to fibre extraction

As has been stated in this book, there are a variety of ways that people have used to extract the fibre from the stems of nettles and so there is no correct, authentic or foolproof way to do it. Different methods also produce different end results. The following information is intended purely to present the basics in order to allow people to try the process and find ways of refining it themselves. Further information about other effective methods of fibre extraction can be found on the Nettles for Textiles website (www.nettlesfortextiles.org.uk).

The fibre on the stem

In simple terms, nettle fibre can be found just below the surface of the skin of the stem. The purpose of the fibre is to strengthen the stem as it grows, until the central core becomes woody as the plant matures.

The individual fibre cells are formed largely of cellulose and can be measured in millimetres. They are loosely bound together with gums and pectins along the length of the stem.

In order to produce fibre that can be spun into a yarn, the fibres need to be separated from the plant material to which it is attached and processed to separate and clean the fibres. The methods that have been used to achieve this are many and varied, depending on local conditions and availability of resources.

As a general rule, the harvest period of nettles for fibre has always taken place at any time from July to October, when they are considered to have reached maturity. After October the stems are considered too woody to process. This harvesting period is, however, questionable. The fibres are one of the first parts of the plants to mature as their function is to strengthen the plant during the early period of its growth. In my opinion, the best time to harvest the stems for fibre is from the end of May and through June when the bast of the stem is still soft and flexible and can be easily peeled away from the central core,[138] though others recommend leaving the stems to weather before harvesting them during the winter.

Decortication

Various tools and machines have been developed to carry out the extraction of fibre from hemp and flax. These range from a simple 'break', which crushes the stems and allows the strands of fibres to be removed from the other plant material, to a fully developed decorticator. A decorticator normally has a system of rollers and combs through which the stems are passed in order to remove the fibre. Unfortunately, those designed for the purpose of decorticating flax and hemp are less effective when removing the fibre from nettles because the mature stems are very hard to crush, are inconsistent in their size, and the nodes where the stems branch cause the strands of fibre to break. It is possible to decorticate 'by hand' by crushing the stems with a hammer (usually after drying them), by trampling or simply breaking with the hand. This should

[138] Edom, G., 2006, *Extraction and Evaluation of Nettle (Urtica dioica) Fibre for Textile End Uses,* MPhil Thesis, De Montfort University, Leicester.

be done carefully so that the fibre strands remain intact and only the central core of the stem is broken. The strands and remaining stem can then be twisted carefully with both hands and the unwanted 'straw' will fall away.

Retting

At some stage in the extraction process, the fibre may be retted, where fibres are separated from the stem through the breakdown of plant matter by microorganisms and moisture. There are two basic methods to achieve this: dew retting and water retting.

Dew Retting

Dew retting takes place when stems are laid out on the ground and fungi break down the soft plant matter, gums and pectins that keep the fibres attached to one another and to the stem.

The weather conditions need to be warm and humid for this process to work successfully. Because it is not possible to control weather systems, this method can be erratic and unreliable. Careful watch needs to be kept on the stems to decide at what stage the plant matter has been sufficiently broken down to enable the removal of the fibres before they themselves are weakened by the action of the fungi. The effectiveness of this method can be improved by drying the stems before retting and by turning them frequently throughout the process.

Water retting

Water retting takes place when the stems are placed in water and the plant matter is broken down by the action of bacteria. This method of retting is often more reliable because conditions are relatively constant. Care must be taken, however, not to leave the stems in the water too long or the fibre is very quickly destroyed. The water retting of stems is generally discouraged because the increase of nutrients added to the water through the breakdown of plant matter can cause eutrophication. In this case it is possible to use a container to ret the stems and many have been tested, such as sheep troughs, baths and barrels. The temperature of the water in the container must be monitored so that it does not become too cold or the bacteria too concentrated. With experience it is possible to develop an 'instinct' for when the fibres are ready.

When hemp and flax fibre was extracted on a relatively large scale in the past, it was common to create retting ponds to retain greater control over the process. They were built on a slope where there was a constant flow of water. Some of these can still be seen today. Where only a small amount of fibre is required, it is sufficient to ret in a pond or stream.

Cleaning the fibre for spinning

An alkali solution is often used to clean the fibres. Wood ash provides a useful source. The fibre that has been pulled away from the stems should be gently heated in the solution, then be cleaned in a sieve using a fast jet of water. When the fibre is dry, any further plant material should fall away during the carding process.

Index

Alsace, 75
Altay Mountains, 24
Amur River, 25
Andersen, Hans Christian, 52-53, 55
Archaeology, 10-12
Austria, 11, 16, 62, 75, 76, 77, 78, 79, 80
Austrian Nettle Society, 76

Backhaus, Emilie, 80
Bacon, Francis, 1
Bashkir Community, 24
Bavaria, 75
Bayerische Nesselfaser-Gesellschaft, 76
Beeston Regis I Hoard, 15
Bella Coola Community (Nuxalk Community), 27
Bering Sea/Strait, 25, 27
Berlin, 77
Beswick, T, 87
Biotechnical Laboratory of the Royal Technical College, Denmark, 80-81
Black Forest, 53
Boehmeria (Ramie or China Grass), 4
  Nivea, 26, 40, 42, 60, 62, 66, 69
  Sylvestrii, 26
Bouché and Grothe, 40, 69-70, 74
Boy Scouts, Denmark, 80
Boys' Voluntary Band, Denmark, 80
Brahetrolleborg, 48
Bredemann, Gustav, 70, 82-84
  Die Grosse Brennessel, 70, 83
Brentwood, 63
British Columbia, 28
Budapest, 76

Calcutta Botanic Gardens, 66
Campbell, Thomas, 46
Canada, 22, 27
Canadian Wood Nettle (*Laportea Canadensis*), 28
Careleton, E. will of, 41, 42
Carrier Community (Dakelh Community), 27
Chelkan Community, 24
Chelmsford Chronicle, 64
China, 29, 62, 69
China Grass (see *Boehmeria*), 66, 69
Commercialisation, 59, 60-61, 63, 66, 71, 73, 82, 89

Copenhagen, 80-81
  Botanical Museum, 73
Coppergate find, 19-20
Cordage, 2, 5, 7, 10, 11, 14, 15, 21, 22, 24, 27, 29
Cotton, 1, 3, 26, 40, 46, 60, 61-62, 63, 64, 65, 74, 75, 79, 83, 89
Crystal Palace, 69
Cultivation, 10, 12-13, 16, 29, 46, 61, 62, 69-70, 74, 76-77, 78, 79, 82-83, 84, 89

Daily Express, 83
Dakelh Community (Carrier Community), 27
Danube Basin, 77
Decortication, *67*, 82, 93-94
Denmark, 14, 16, *17*, 18, 47, 48, 52, 60, 62, 72, 73, 80-81
Deulin, Charles, 54
Dodwell, Christina, 21
Draper's Dictionary, 41
Dundee Advertiser, 45

East India Companies, 60
East Jutland, 62
Elizabeth I, 3
Elster, Johannes, 82
Esparto Grass, 84
Essex, 63
Etymology, 4-7
Evens Community, 25

Fensmark, Mrs. Elna, 80
Fairy tales, 52-57
Fasernessel (*Urtica dioica L. convar. Fibra*), 89
Fibre extraction, 3, 12, 14, 24, 25, 26, 28, 29, 32-33, 37, 41, 42, 47, 48, 67, 61, 62, 69-70, 74-75, 76, 77, 79, 80-81, 82, 84, 85, 88, 89, 92-94
Fibre identification, 10, 12, 13, 14, 16
Fibre Nettle (Fasernessel), 83
Figat, Mrs., 48
Fileuse d'Orties, La, (The Nettle Spinner), 53-54
Finland, 23
Finno-Ugrian language, 23
Flanders, 53-54
Flax, 1, 9, 12-13, 14, 16, 39, 46, 47, 48, 51, 56, 59, 61, 63, 64, 65, 79, 93, 95
Flensborg, 73
Fluringen, 18

France, 60, 61, 62, 66
Funnelbeaker Culture, 14

Gebruder Uebel, Adorf, Vogtland, 82
German Nettle Industry, 73
Germany, 40, 53, 60-61, 66, *68*, 69-70, 73, 75-79, 82-84
Girardinia, 4
  diversifolia, 29
Gitskan Community (Gitxsan Community), 27
Glemmen Chruch, Ostfold, 72
Gravis, A, *91*
Great Exhibition, The, 21, 66, 69
Grew, Nehemiah, 45
Grimm Brothers, 42
Grove, H., His Majesty's Consul, Moscow, 79

Haida Community, 27
Hakluyt, Richard, 1
Hald, Margrethe, 11, 14, 23, 47, 48, 52, 59, 60
Halkomelem Community, 27
Hamburg, 82
  Institute of Applied Botany, 83
Hanamaki Mountains, 32, 37
Hawaii, 29
Hehn, Victor, 1
Hemp, 1, 21, 23, 24, 25, 39, 47, 48-49, 59, 63, 64, 65, 93, 95
Henry VIII, 3
Hesquiaht Community, 28
Høeg, Professor Arbo, 72
Hoffberg, Carl Fredrik, 47
Holland (see Netherlands), 62
Horsham, 42, *43*, 44
Hugo, Victor, 39
Hungary, 52, 76, 83

Ice Man (Ötzi), 11
India, 29, 62
In-SHUCK-ch Community (Lower Lillooet Community), 27
Italy, 11
Itelmen Community, 21, 25
Iwate Prefecture, 32

Japan, 22, 25, 26-27, 32-38, *34-38*

Kamchadal Community, 21, 26
Kamchatka River, 25
Karelia, 23
Kärnten-Steiermark region, 16
Khabarovsky region, 25
Khanty Community, 21, 23-24
Knittle (Nittle), 5, 7
Knox, Captain Charles, 53
Køie, Dr. M, 16, 18
Koryak Community, 21
Krasheninnikov, 25
Kumandin Community, 24
Kvalsund find, 18
Kwakiutl Community (Kwakwata' wakw Community), 27
Kwakwata' wakw Community (Kwakiutl Community), 27

Lang, Andrew, 54
Laportea, 4, 32, 45, 46
  canadensis, (Canadian Wood Nettle) 28, 29, 60
  cuspidata, 26, 32, 33, *34*, 37
  macrostachya, 32, 37
Latham, R. E., 41
Leeds, 66
Leipzig, 61
Linen, 1, 3, 24, 39, 40, 45, 46, 47, 48, 49, 51, 59, 72, 73, 74
Little Gidding, Huntingdonshire, 2
Lower Lillooet Community (In-SHUCK-ch Community), 27
Lower Thompson Community (Nlaka'pamux Community), 27, 28

Madagascar, 29
Magic for Women, 48-49
Magnus, Albertus, 40-41
Mansi Community, 23
Mary Queen of Scots, 3
Mears, Ray, 13-14
Menominee Community, 29
Metcalfe, C. R., 71, 85
Middle Ages, 18
Milwaukee, 29
Mishnah, Treatise Sabbath, 9
Mordvinians, 23
Moscow, 79
Munich, 76
Musée de l'Armee, Paris, 3

Napoleonic Wars, 48, 86
Napoleon's soldiers, 3-4
National Museum, Copenhagen, 24, 85, 86, 93
Nauen, 77, 79
Nebraska, 29
Nepal, 29
Nesselanbau Gesellschaft, *67*, 76
Nesselfaserverwertungs-Gesellschaft, 76
Nestorius, 22-23
Netherlands (Holland), 64
Netting and nets, 1, 4, 10, 11, 21, 23, 24, 25, 26, 27
Nettle Family (*Urticaceae*), 4, 22, 29, 62, 88
Nettlecloth, 1, 5, 18-19, 23, 39, 40, 41, 42, 44, 46, 48, 59, 60, 61, 62-63, 72, 73-74
Nettles for Textiles website, 92
Nettle stuff, 5
Niederwald, 77
Nielsdatter, Karen, 73, *81*
Nisga Community (Nisg'a Community), 27
Nittle (Knittle), 5
Nivkh Community, 25
Nlaka'pamux Community (Lower Thompson Community), 27, 28
Nootka Community (Nuu-chah-nulth Community), 27
Nørre Sandegaard, 18
Norsk Folkemuseum, 72
North America, 22, 27
Norway, 18, 19, 72

98

Nuu-chah-nulth Community (Nootka Community), 27
Nuxalk Community (Bella Coola Community), 27

Oakley, F. I., 1, 9, 59
Oakes, J., 21
Ob, River, 23
Ojibwe Community, 21, 29
Okhotsk, Sea of, 25
Olona (*Touchardia latifolia*), 29
Omaha Community, 29
Orissa, 1
Orochi Community, 25
Oseburg Burial Ship, 19
Ostjak Community, 11
Ötzi (Ice Man), 11
Överflödsförordningar (sumptuary laws), 60

Paper (fibre for), 65, 71, 84-85
Partsch, Anna Maria Beata, 73
Picardy, 61
Plying, 24, 28, 32
Polarised light microscopy, 16
Propaganda, 3, 70, 76, 78, 88
Pyrenees, 1

Rackham, Oliver, 54
Ramie (see *Boehmeria nivea*), 9, 40, 42, 60, 62-63, 66, 67, 69, 78
Red Fairy Book, The, 54
Retting, 1, 18, 32, 47, 53, 64, 75, 80, 94-95
Richter, Oswald, 94-95, 98, 98-99
Riewe, R., 21
Roxburgh, William, 66
Royal Botanical Gardens, Kew, 71, 85
Russia, 22-23, 84

Saanich Community, 28
Sagai Tartar Community, 24
Sailor's Pocket Book, 5
St. Viby, Hindsholm, 73
Sakhalin, Island of, 25
Sakiori, 27
Saxony, 62
Scandinavia, 16, 20, 47-49
Schiller, I., 59
Schleswig Holstein region, 73
Schlichten, G. W., *67*
Scotch Cloth, 42, 45-46
Scotland, 42, 46
Siberia, 11, 21, 22, 24-26, 27
Silesia, 75
Silk, 1, 26, 60, 66, 87
Six Swans, The, 52
Smith, Edward, 63-65
Smith, H. H., 21
Society of Arts, 64
Society of Œconomy, Haarlem, 64
South Carolina, State of, 65
Special war purposes, 84-85
Spencer, Violet, 71
Squamish Community, 27
Stockholm, 83

Straits Salish Community, 27, 28
Sweden, 60
Swedish Ethnological Archives, 53
Sweet Track arrowhead, 13-14
Switzerland, 18

Tabby weave, 16, *17*
Teltow Canal, 77
Thompson Community, 27, 28
Tlingit Community, 27
Touchardia latifolia (Olona), 29
Tsimshian Community, 27
Tullner Edelnessel, 74

Udegey Community, 25
Ul'chi Community, 25
United States, 27, 28, 65, 84
Ural Mountains, 23, 24
Urera oligoloba, 29
Urtica cannabina, 22
Urtica dioica L. convar. *fibra* (Die Fasernessel), 89
Urtica gracilis, 28, 65
Urtica holosericea, 28
Urtica lyalli, 28
Urtica nivea, 66
Urtica serra, 28
Urtica tenacissima, 66
Urtica thunbergiana, 26
Urtica whitlowii, 65
Urticaceae (Nettle Family), 4, 29, 62
Uttley, Alison, 51

Valley of the Mourg, The, 53
Vancouver Island, 28
Voldofte Grave find, 16, *17*, 18
Volga, River, 23

West Sussex, 42, 44
West Washington Communities, 27
Whitehorse Hill burial, 14-15
Whitlow, Charles, 65
Wild Swans, The, 52-53, 55-57
Wilkinson, Lady, 45
Wright & Co, L.W., Messrs., *67*, 69
Williams, Dai, 11
Wogul Community, 11
Wright, Mr. Ernest, *67*
Woodgate, Michael, of Horsham, 42, *43*, 44
Wool, 3, 10, 18, 19, 23, 61, 72
World War, First, 74-79, 82
World War, Second, 23, 79, 82, 83-95
World's Paper Trade Review, 84

Zehlendorf, 77, 79